ETHICALITY AND IMAGINATION

THE COLLECTED WRITINGS OF JOHN SALLIS

Volume I/25

ETHICALITY AND IMAGINATION

On Luminous Abodes

John Sallis

Indiana University Press

This book is a publication of

Indiana University Press
Office of Scholarly Publishing
Herman B Wells Library 350
1320 East 10th Street
Bloomington, Indiana 47405 USA

iupress.org

Manufactured in the United States of America

Collected Writings of John Sallis printing 2022

Cataloging information is available from the Library of Congress.

ISBN 978-0-253-06398-4 (hardback)
ISBN 978-0-253-06399-1 (paperback)
ISBN 978-0-253-06400-4 (ebook)

To Jerry

Once Again and Always

But if a man would be alone
let him look at the stars.

—Ralph Waldo Emerson, *Nature*

Contents

Prefatory Note

THIS BOOK BELONGS to the series that also includes *Force of Imagination* and *Logic of Imagination*. While its tonality remains that of imagination, its primary theme is that expressed in the word ἦθος.

I am deeply grateful to Nancy Fedrow for her exemplary assistance in the preparation of this book. Thanks also to Peter Hanly for his invaluable editorial assistance.

Boston
June 2022

ETHICALITY AND IMAGINATION

1   Ventriloquies of Origin

"BUT COME, HEAR my speech, for learning increases wisdom. As I said before in declaring the limits of my speech, I shall speak double. At one time they grew to be one alone from many; at another they grew apart to be many out of one— fire, water, earth, and the lofty expanse of air, destructive strife apart from them, equal in every direction, and love among them, equal in height and width. Gaze on her with your mind; do not sit with eyes dazzled by her who is supposed to be innate even in mortal limbs. Because of her they think friendly thoughts and accomplish harmonious deeds, calling her by the names of Joy and Aphrodite. She is perceived by no mortal man as she circles among them. But you must listen to the undeceptive ordering of my speech. All these are equal and of the same age. Each honorably guards its abode, and they prevail in turn as time rolls round."[1]

In this speech, this μῦθος, itself limited, Empedocles addresses Pausanias, his pupil and lover. The word rendered as—that is, reduced to—*abode* is ἦθος. Empedocles is instructing Pausanias about the four roots: that each of the four has its own ἦθος, its own abode, its own region, its own τόπος, which it guards against encroachment by any other of the four. It guards its abode because of what it itself is. Yet, in turn, what it is, its character, is determined by its abode: earth cannot abide in the abode of air but only in the abode proper to it. Nonetheless, strife always poses the threat of unlimited encroachment, and thus each of the four roots must guard itself. Because fire is fire and not earth, water, or air, it must guard the abode within which it belongs. It is likewise for each of the four. When each persists in its own abode, there is love among them, each ordered to the others, Aphrodite circling among them. The character of each—and *character* also translates ἦθος[2]—cannot be thought except in its belonging to its abode, to its proper ἦθος.

* * *

"There is an ancient tale, one told long ago. The tale is this. It is said that he who dies a violent death, after having lived thoughtfully and free, is filled with wrath

---

1. Empedocles, Fragment B17.
2. Because of the multiplicity and range of the lexical meanings that constitute the matrix of the word ἦθος, there can be no question of translating it by a single term. The complexity of this matrix becomes all the more evident when these meanings are taken not merely as designated by single terms but rather as emerging from discursive contexts in which they function in a determining way.

toward his slayer when newly slain. Filled with fear and dread on account of his own violent end, and seeing his own murderer going about in his own habitual haunts, he is horror-stricken. Being himself disturbed, he does all he can, having memory as an ally, to disturb the perpetrator and his doings. That is why the perpetrator must go away for a full year, in all its seasons, and vacate all the domestic places throughout all parts of his native land. And if the one who has died should be a foreigner, the perpetrator must also keep away from the foreigner's country for the same amount of time."[3]

The Athenian retells this ancient story in order to underwrite the law being proposed regarding the punishment or purification of one who, as in the case of the perpetrator in the story, kills a free man involuntarily. The entire story is centered around the reference to the habitual haunts of the man who is slain, which the slayer then goes about. It is to prevent the perpetrator from abiding in these haunts, while the slain man is still filled with horror, that he is legally obligated to go away from all the places that had been habitual haunts of the slain man. *Habitual haunt* is a hendiadys that translates ἦθος. It is echoed by the expression *domestic place*, which translates οἰκεῖος τόπος. It is evident that here ἦθος means primarily *abode*. Yet, it has the sense not just of a place that one might occupy but of a place where one such as the slain man would habitually have abided. It is a place frequented so regularly that it has become habitual to come there.

The legal obligation is the same if the victim happens to be a foreigner. The man who has slain him is to be barred from the foreign land that is native to the one slain. He is obligated to keep away from the foreigner's country. Here—quite remarkably—the word χώρα occurs, translated as *country*, that is, as the land to which one belongs. The passage as a whole thus establishes an affiliation between ἦθος, τόπος, and χώρα.

* * *

"First of all, the deathless gods who dwell on Olympus made a golden race of mortal men who lived in the age of Cronos when he was reigning in the sky [οὐρανός]. . . . They had all good things, for the fruitful land [ἄρουρα] bore them fruit abundantly."

"But after the earth had covered this race . . . then those who dwell on Olympus made a second race, which was of silver and less noble by far. It was like the golden race neither in its nature nor in its understanding. A child born into the silver race was brought up at his mother's side and was a simpleton who merely played childishly in the home. When those of the silver race were full grown and reached their prime, they lived only a short time and that in sorrow because of their foolishness; they could not refrain from violence against one another. They

---

3. Plato, *Laws* 865 d–e.

would not serve the immortals nor sacrifice on the sacred altars of the blessed ones, as is right for humans to do according to their abode. Then Zeus, son of Cronos, was angry and covered them over because they would not pay honor to the sacred gods who dwell on Olympus."[4]

The golden race abided under the reign of Cronos; as such, they were bounded by the sky, and their abidance was ruled by the god whose domain was the sky. Thus bounded, they abided on the earth from which they received all the things needed by mortal life. Their abidance was set between earth and sky.

While in Hesiod's account the word ἦθος occurs only in relation to the silver race, its sense also implicitly governs the account of the golden race. Yet, because those belonging to the golden race abided in peace between uranic rule and the bounteous earth, they were not subject to demands by the gods nor to the consequences of not abiding by such demands. On the other hand, for those belonging to the silver race—ruled by angry Zeus rather than peaceful Cronos—it was required that, on pain of suffering retribution by the gods, they sacrifice according to their abode (κατὰ ἤθεα), that is, in the manner prescribed in the πόλις in which they abided. Yet, to perform sacrifices in this manner is tantamount to observing the customs of that πόλις as regards sacrifices. Thus, in the phrase κατὰ ἤθεα, the word ἦθος signifies both the place where those of the silver race abided, their πόλις, and the customs of that πόλις as regards sacrifices to the gods. In the word ἦθος the two meanings are brought together and their coherence is affirmed. For those no longer abiding peacefully between earth and sky, indeed for all that have suffered the decline from the perfection of the golden race—for all that come thereafter—an abode is no mere place; it is not simply a location where mortals live. Rather, it is a place in which all who reside there are bound by custom yet also oriented and directed by it. To abide in a πόλις is to be submitted to its imperatives. Thus, the word ἦθος in its double meaning attests that abode and custom belong together.

And yet, Hesiod's account also points beyond the connection that an abode sustains with custom. For, according to his account of the golden race, their abode is delimited by earth and sky, and it is highly questionable whether in such an abode the bonds of custom would be necessary or even appropriate. Even if mortals fail to abide by this delimitation, this very oblivion to earth and sky as elemental would be constitutive of all latter day abodes.

* * *

"Now if haply there chances to be nearby one who knows bird cries, then, hearing our bitter passion, he will fancy that he hears the voice of Metis, Tereus' sad wife, the hawk-chased nightingale. For she, constrained to leave her green leaves,

---

4. Hesiod, *Works and Days* 121–39.

laments and longs for her abode; and with her lament she blends the tale of her child's doom, of how he was killed by her through her perverse wrath."[5]

Here the chorus lets the suppliant maiden be imaginatively transformed into Metis, who took revenge on her evil husband by killing, dismembering, cooking, and serving to him their young son. Fleeing, she was pursued by Tereus, and just as he prepared to kill her, the gods rescued her by turning her into a nightingale. Even before her fabulous metamorphosis and especially afterwards when she could sing as a nightingale sings, her song is a lament for her abode, for her ἦθος. The thought of her abode evokes mourning for what is now irretrievably lost. In her flight she calls up in memory an image of her abode as a place of shelter. So, an abode can shelter as a child is sheltered in the home, protected from perilous exposure to the world beyond. And yet, just as it shelters, an abode can be violated and become the scene of the most heinous deed, murdering one's own child, desecrating his remains. In sheltering there is always the possibility of intervening violence, and insofar as it is a violence committed within the very shelter provided by one's abode, it is all the more violent.

* * *

"The sun rose on the flawless brimming sea into a sky all brazen—to shine upon the immortals and also on mortals across the grain-giving farmland. The voyagers now came to Pylos, strong-founded citadel of Neleus. On the shore black bulls were being sacrificed to the dark-haired god who makes the island tremble: there were nine settlements of them, each five hundred strong, and they led out nine bulls each for sacrifice. Now they tasted the entrails, and the thighbones in fat lay on the altars burning for the god. Here the voyagers put in, furled sail, and moored the ship. Telemachus stepped out of the ship, but Athena went first, and it was the gray-eyed goddess Athena who first spoke to him: 'Telemachus, there is no need for modesty; for this was why you sailed on the open sea, to find news of your father, where the great earth hides him, what fate he has met with.'"

Then, in praise of the poet of poets: "Homer, who is worthy of praise for many other things, is also the only poet who is not ignorant of what part he should play in his own poems. For an epic poet should speak in his own person as little as possible; otherwise he fails to imitate to the extent that he fails to impersonate. The other poets put themselves forward throughout their poems and imitate but little and seldom. Homer, on the other hand, after a brief introduction, immediately brings on a man or a woman or some other character, never without character, but all having character."[6]

---

5. Aeschylus, *The Suppliant Maidens* 58–67.
6. Homer, *Odyssey* 3.1–16; Aristotle, *Poetics* 1460a5–11.

That for which Aristotle bestows such praise on Homer is attested again and again in the Homeric epics. Homer knows not to speak in his own person except in a brief introduction that sets the scene for the mimetic narrative that follows. The openings are among the most celebrated passages: "under the rosy fingers of the young dawn"; "when primal dawn spread on the eastern sky her fingers of rosy light"; "dawn arose from the couch of her reclining"; "now dawn the yellow-robed scattered over all the earth."[7] Yet, regardless of whether, in any particular Book, they open in precisely this way, the introductions are devoted primarily to describing the setting and the circumstances of those who are to be dramatically represented thereafter. Then, with the introduction completed, individual characters come upon the scene, perhaps to do battle but more often to speak. Thus it is that Telemachus and Athena step forth from the ship, and the goddess speaks to the son of Odysseus. Hence, as Aristotle describes it, Homer brings on a man or a woman, or some other character—in this case a man and a goddess—a character who is never without character, but who has character. In this description the word *character*, in each of its three occurrences, translates a form of ἦθος. In the first occurrence it designates a *dramatis persona*, a character who, immediately following the introduction, comes upon the scene, in this case Athena and Telemachus. Yet, in the other two occurrences it refers to character in the sense of a person's—or a character's—innate and/or developed, enduring temperament. We—in our time—could perhaps speak of a person's "moral quality" but—to sustain the return toward the origin—it would be necessary, once this phrase has said what it can to us, to cross it out or efface it.

Although in Aristotle's eulogy to Homer the word ἦθος occurs only in the sense of *character*, the scene of the action in the Homeric passage implicitly portrays two other senses. Homer brings two characters (not without character, having character) onto the scene, which displays both the shore of Pylos where the citizens are gathered and, indirectly, the custom of this πόλις by which is prescribed the sacrifice of black bulls, nine of them in each of nine settlements within the confines of Pylos. Thus, Aristotle's rendering of ἦθος as *character* can be conjoined with the tacit Homeric portrayal of ἦθος as *abode* and as *custom*.

How is it that in pairing these two passages—in other ways as well—there is broached a conjunction of three senses of ἦθος? How, in general, do these senses belong together? In whatever form this conjunction may be eventually determined, it already portends a basic schema governing the semantic spread of the word ἦθος and constituting its full matrix.

The very sense of abode entails that it is inhabited by certain characters, by one or more individuals. In the epic or in the theatre, these characters are presented in their particular or specific character, often as displaying a unique or a

---

7. Homer, *Odyssey* 8.1;2.1–2;5.1. Homer, *Iliad* 8.1.

typical character. In the specific character they display a particular abode. In the Homeric epic they are brought forth (as Telemachus and Athena stepped out of the ship) as soon as the poet has described the abode in which their speech and action will take place. In Greek drama they step forth onto the stage, which represents an abode, and in their words and deeds they reveal the character of the character they are impersonating.

In one's abode—whether it be οἰκία, κοινωνία, or πόλις—one has one's bearings; one has a sense of how to carry out one's concerns with things and others within the abode. These bearings are supported by directives, often covert, that in turn are sustained by the customs instituted and observed in the abode. It is the customs of one's abode that prescribe the ways in which, for example, sacrifices are to be offered up to the gods by the assemblage of those who abide within the abode.

Still further, the abode in which one lives and the customs observed in that abode are instrumental in shaping one's character. There is no such thing as character in the abstract; rather, character necessarily accommodates the demands of customs and of the abode to which the customs belong. Even one who eludes or refuses such accommodation still displays a character that to some degree is determined—even if negatively—by these demands. Abode and character are knitted together concretely. They do not meld together into an indifferent unity; rather, in their very distinctness, in their difference, each reaches out to the other along multiple concrete paths. What one is, one's character, is never entirely independent of where one abides.

And yet, one's abode is not limited, is not definitively circumscribed, by the community or the πόλις to which one belongs. In its greatest expanse, ἦθος denotes the abode shared by all humans, the domain delimited by earth and sky or, equally, by sea and sun. The Homeric passage inscribes the arrival of the characters on the shore of Pylos within designations of this broadest expanse. The first word of the passage (the first word of Book 3) is ἠέλιος (= ἥλιος); in the same sentence the word οὐρανός (sky) occurs. Both words refer to the upper limit from which light is bestowed on the immortals and grain is made to grow from the land (ἄρουρα) for mortals. Moreover, when at the end of the passage the goddess speaks, she reminds Telemachus that he has sailed over the sea to discover where his father has been covered by the great earth (γαῖα).

* * *

"'What you suggest is correct,' he said. 'And it is clear to everyone that there is no πόλις more wretched than one under a tyranny and none happier than one under a kingship.' 'And about these same things, as they exist in the men,' I said, 'would I also be correct in suggesting that that man should be deemed fit to judge them who is able with his thought to creep into someone's character and see through it—a man who is not like a child looking from outside and overwhelmed by the tyrannic pomp set up as a façade for those outside, but who rather sees through it adequately?'"

Elsewhere, the words of another Athenian:

"Then is it not in all these that we are of such kind: spirited anger, erotic desire, insolence, ignorance, love of gain, cowardice; and these also: wealth, beauty, strength, and everything that drives a person out of his wits so that he is beside himself with pleasure? And for the purpose, first, of providing an inexpensive and comparatively harmless test of these conditions, and, secondly, of affording practice in them, what more suitable device can we mention than wine with the playful testing—provided that it is employed at all carefully? . . . [It is] with the aid of Dionysus and his festive vision . . . [that one] can discover the character of a man's soul. . . . Indeed in this respect we believe that neither the Cretans nor any other people would disagree that this is a decent way of testing one another, one that in cheapness, safety, and speed is superior to all other tests."[8]

Socrates's contention is that the able judge of men is the one who has the capacity to penetrate the disguises, the external façade, so as to reach into a man's *character*, to creep into his ἦθος. Here the word clearly signifies a person's enduring condition, his temperament, his inwardness. The judge is the one who, through his thinking, can look through the outer man, through his exterior bearing, so as to discern his inner ἦθος.

In the Platonic dialogues the paradigm—other than Socrates himself—of such penetrating vision is, paradoxically, Alcibiades in his relation to Socrates. Not only does Alcibiades see beyond Socrates's ugliness into his noble character, but also he proclaims that it is likewise with Socrates's speech. He compares Socrates's speech to the Silenus figures, which on the outside are—like Silenus— quite ugly but which can be opened to reveal their treasures within. Like these figures, Socrates's speech appears externally to be absurd, indeed laughable, and yet, just as the little figures open so as to expose what lies within, so when Socrates's words are opened and one gazes into their inner sense, they prove to be the most meaningful and the most godly.[9]

The able judge, if sufficiently thoughtful, will, then, be able to discern the inner character, the ἦθος, which for others less thoughtful remains hidden from view. Yet, lacking such an able judge, there is another way to discover the ἦθος of a man's soul, a way that is inexpensive, safe, and speedy. One can borrow from Dionysus his festive vision; in that festival the inner man, his ἦθος, will be

---

8. Plato, *Republic* 576e–577a; Plato, *Laws* 649d.
9. See Plato, *Symposium* 221e–222a.

exposed, opened up like the figures of Silenus. The proverbial saying regarding wine and truth would thus be put into practice.

* * *

"Shall we not legislate that, in the first place, no children under the age of eighteen may taste wine at all. We will teach that one should not pour fire into the fire that is already in the body and the soul until they have taken up their tasks, thus guarding against the mad condition of the youth. After this, the young man under the age of thirty will be permitted to drink wine in moderation, but he must abstain from drunkenness and heavy drinking. As a man approaches forty, he is to share in the enjoyment of the common meals and invoke Dionysus, above all the other gods, at what is at once a celebration of the mysteries and the play of older men, which he has bestowed on humans as a potion [φάρμακον] that heals the austerity of old age, that thereby we may become young again and that, by forgetting the despondency, the soul may have its bearing, its manner, (ἦθος) turned from harder to softer, so that it becomes more malleable, like iron when it is plunged into fire."[10]

Wine is the fire of the soul. The Athenian declares that since the youth are already afire with the flame of their mad condition, one should not add fuel—that is, more fire—to the fire that is already in their body and their soul. The law to be enacted will require of the youth the discipline of total abstinence. For those between eighteen and thirty, the discipline is relaxed somewhat, though their drinking must be done in proper measure. But then, as they approach forty, the constraints are removed almost entirely.[11] Dionysus is invoked and brings to the playful celebrations of the old men his magic potion, a φάρμακον that in this case has primarily—though not perhaps entirely—the sense of medicine or remedy.[12] To souls in which the fire of youthful madness has been extinguished, leaving the soul—like the aged body—despondent as the prospect of death looms ever greater, wine comes to bring relief. It brings about a forgetting, which could never be tolerated in the youth, who, with tasks to take up, must cultivate the gaining of knowledge, not its loss through forgetting. The fire of wine also softens the soul, relieving it of the inflexibility that age will have brought on. By this means,

---

10. Plato, *Laws* 666a–c.
11. There is a passage in which the Athenian condemns drunkenness, with which, however, drinking in the Dionysian gatherings is, it seems, not to be conflated. He observes that when drunk, a man is clumsy and also is likely to beget offspring whose bodies and character (ἦθος) are deformed (*Laws* 775c–d).
12. The potion that Socrates is compelled to drink on his last day is, throughout the *Phaedo*, designated by the word φάρμακον. It is not uncommon for the dual sense by which the word designates both remedy and poison to be in play in particular discourses. Especially where this is the case, the consequences are far-reaching.

wine allows the older men to recapture their youth; its fire sets aflame the souls in which otherwise no fire remains. The fire of wine would, then, also restore—if only temporarily—the mad condition characteristic of the youth. Wherever Dionysus was present, some form of madness was not far away. In *The Bacchae*, Dionysus's power to instill madness is dramatically presented: not only was there madness in his followers, the Maenads, but, in more destructive form, madness was brought on among the women of Thebes, who tore Pentheus the King to pieces limb from limb. But to the old men of whom the Athenian speaks, Dionysus would be kind, bringing them only relief and rejuvenation. Like iron plunged into fire, the bearing (ἦθος) of the older men is transformed; their disposition is, if only for a time, rendered playful, almost as though their youth had been regained. Wine lets their manner become again what it once was, reversing the advance of time.

In this context ἦθος has the sense of a bearing or manner that, by the fire of wine, can be transformed into a very different bearing. Thus, in distinction from character, which endures with only minimal change, bearing is, in this instance, pluralized in a unique way: one kind of bearing can undergo transformation into another quite opposed to it, as age is opposed to youth, as hard is opposed to soft.

The bearing of the older men at any particular time is shaped not only by nature[13] but also in a manner that in a certain respect runs counter to nature, to the aging to which all are, by nature, exposed. Furthermore, the fiery disposition that wine can confer on the older men is brought about in a way that is the very opposite of what is required of the youth. Whereas the madness of youth requires that discipline be imposed, the rejuvenation of the older men requires that this very discipline be relinquished.

* * *

"'So, Glaucon,' I said, 'isn't this why the rearing in music is most sovereign? Because rhythm and harmony most of all insinuate themselves into the innermost part of the soul and most vigorously lay hold of it in bringing grace with them; and they make a man graceful if he is correctly reared, if not, the opposite. Furthermore it is sovereign because the man properly reared on rhythm and harmony would have the sharpest sense for what's been left out and for what is not beautifully crafted and for what is not beautifully begotten by nature. And due to his having the right kind of dislikes, he would praise all the truly beautiful things and, taking pleasure in them and receiving them into his soul, he would be reared on them and would himself become beautiful and

---

13. In another passage in the *Laws* dealing with the relation between character and virtue, the Athenian refers to those who, though not believing in the gods, possess *by nature* a just character (ἦθος φύσει . . . δίκαιον) (908b).

good. He would blame and hate the ugly in the correct way while he is still young, before he is able to receive [λαβεῖν] λόγος. And when the λόγος comes, the man who is reared in this way will take most delight in it, recognizing it on account of its being akin. . . . So in the name of the gods, is it as I say: we'll never be musical . . . before we recognize the looks of moderation, courage, liberality, magnificence, and all their kin . . .?' 'Quite necessarily,' he said. 'Then,' I said, 'if the beautiful character that is in the soul (ἐν τε τῇ ψυχῇ καλὰ ἤθη ἐνόντα) and those that are in accord with these looks should ever coincide in anyone, with both partaking of the same model, wouldn't that be the most beautiful sight for one who is able to see?'"[14]

Socrates is the advocate of music as enabling education (παιδεία) at all levels. In a young man, rhythm and harmony come to be doubled in the innermost part of his soul. Music gradually instills character in his soul; it promotes grace, which, in turn, inculcates a sense by which to discern whatever—whether produced by τέχνη or engendered by nature—is not beautiful. Yet, this development of character also grants the young man a first intimation of the beauty that lies beyond the fabrication of τέχνη and the begotten of nature. This intimation prepares him to receive the λόγος and thereby awakens his receptiveness to the looks. His ascent reaches its culmination when his beautiful character comes into accord with his vision of the looks. Music casts the soul upward, shaping its character so as to open it to λόγος and to the looks; and ultimately it fosters accord with the looks themselves, realizing its kinship with them. Thereby, he would, in the end, become truly musical.

In Socrates's discourse on music, ἦθος designates character, the formation of which in the youth can be furthered through music, since the grace that belongs to character is imparted by musical rhythm and harmony.

*   *   *

"'But these marvels do not urge things on as wine does. But if people were to have, with an aulos accompaniment, dancing figures depicting the Graces, the Horae, and the Nymphs, I believe that they would be far less wearied themselves and that the charms of the symposium would be greatly enhanced.' 'By Zeus, Socrates,' replied the Syracusan, 'you speak beautifully, and I will bring sights that will delight you.' So the Syracusan withdrew amid applause. Socrates introduced a new, strange discourse. . . . 'Of love we should not be forgetful, since we all belong to his band of revelers. For I cannot name a time when I was not in love with someone, and I know that Charmides here has gained many lovers and has in some instances felt desire himself. And Critobulos, though even yet the object of love, is already beginning to have desire for others. And Niceratus too, so I hear,

---

14. Plato, *Republic* 401d–e, 402b–d.

is in love with his wife and is loved in return. And as for Hermogenes, who of us does not know that he is pining away with love for beauty and goodness? Do you not see how serious his brow is, how calm his gaze, how modest his speech, how gentle his voice, how cheerful his demeanor?'"[15]

The Xenophontic banquet is not entirely unlike Plato's. There is the extravagant praise of love personified as a god, and there are the erotic words and gestures among those present. There are references to the playing of the aulos as accompaniment to dancing figures, and there is acknowledgment of the potency of wine. But in the end, indeed precisely at the end, it is utterly different: in place of the entrance of the drunken Alcibiades with the aulos-playing girl and the general commotion and drunkenness that eventually ensues, Xenophon's *Symposium* concludes with the appearance of Dionysus and Ariadne, whose tender gestures of love so impress those observing the couple that all except Socrates and a few others go off to their wife or in search of a wife. On the other hand, Xenophon's portrayal of Socrates resembles in many—though by no means all—respects that in Plato's *Symposium*. According to Xenophon, he is profuse in his praise of love and is attentive to the erotic relations of those around him. He is not adverse to a kind of erotic playfulness in speech, as in his exchange with Antisthenes. Asked by Socrates whether he is in love with anyone, Antisthenes declares: "I am madly in love with you!" Socrates's response is an ironic imitation of the evasive words typical of a beloved approached by his lover. Bantering and laughing, he says: "Don't bother me now. I'm busy with other things."[16]

For the most part, Socrates's praise of love is instantiated by his identification of the erotic relation of those present at the banquet. Some love boys, some love women; some are boys who have or who do not yet have their lovers. Hermogenes is the exception: Socrates observes that he is pining away with love for beauty and goodness. Socrates's observation leaves it undecidable whether the missing object of Hermogenes's love is beauty and goodness as such or a beautiful and good boy or woman. Socrates does say, perhaps ironically, that Hermogenes—whose name means *progeny of Hermes*, though in fact he was a bastard—enjoys friendship with the gods. What is most striking is Socrates's description of the visible and audible signs that he is in love, even if in the absence of the object of his love. Socrates calls attention to the seriousness of Hermogenes's brow, the calmness of his gaze, the modesty of his words, the gentleness of his voice; and then, finally and most decisively, bringing all these qualities together, he speaks of the cheerfulness of Hermogenes's demeanor. Here the word *demeanor* translates ἦθος. With this word Socrates gathers together all the other capacities through which Hermogenes appears in his particular manner: his brow, his gaze, his words, and

---

15. Xenophon, *Symposium* 7.5–8.3.
16. Ibid., 8.4.

his voice. The ways in which he thus appears all belong to his outward bearing, to the various respects in which he presents himself to the vision and audition of others. All these modes of appearance come together in his ἦθος; and the qualities of these come together in the cheerfulness of his ἦθος. These qualities and the ἦθος in which they are gathered make up his outer appearance, his outward bearing. Thus, ἦθος no longer has the sense expressed in the word *character*—not, at least, insofar as character is regarded as lying hidden away in the soul. Rather, ἦθος is corporeal, the look projected or the sound produced by an embodied being.

On the other hand, ἦθος in this sense is not necessarily detached from the soul and the character that belongs to it. A person's ἦθος may express his character; a person's words, for instance, or the sound of his voice may disclose whether he is one to be trusted, whether his character has the quality of trustworthiness. A person's ἦθος may also express states of the soul that are less permanent and more subject to external affection. Thus it is that Hermogenes's ἦθος expresses the peculiar love that he has for beauty and goodness. In this manner, ἦθος, even in the sense of outward bearing, can be a sign pertaining to a person's inwardness. As Socrates tells Hermogenes in Plato's *Cratylus*, the body is the signifier of the soul.[17]

* * *

"That is just how it is, dear Phaedrus. But it is much nobler to be serious about these matters and use the τέχνη of dialectic, choosing a suitable soul and planting and sowing within it discourses with knowledge—discourses which are capable of helping themselves as well as the man who planted them and which are not barren but produce seed from which more discourses grow in the character of others. Such discourses make the seed forever undying and render the man who has them as happy as any human being can be."[18]

Socrates's praise of dialectic is, at once, in praise also of discourse, of λόγος. Dialectic is the τέχνη by which we are enabled to plant and sow discourses within the soul. The parallel is most fitting: these discourses, planted like seed, have the capacity, again like seed, to produce other discourses that, once again like seed, spread abroad into other souls. More precisely, that in which these spermatic discourses grow is the character of others, their ἦθος. As in other passages, ἦθος has here indeed the sense expressed in the word *character*. But what is remarkable and is distinctive about this passage is the way in which character mutates into a fertile soil in which the seeds of discourse are planted. What Socrates explains to

---

17. See Plato, *Cratylus* 400c.
18. Plato, *Phaedrus* 276e–277a.

dear Phaedrus is that ἦθος is the site where λόγοι reproduce and are strewn, that is, disseminated."Ηθος is, for λόγοι, the site of dissemination.

* * *

In these words inscribed by figures across the expanse leading from Homer to Plato and Aristotle and here given voice, ἦθος displays an extensive and indeed remarkable semantic itinerary. In ever varying guises its sense ranges across a spectrum: from the abode of each of the elements to abode as permeated by custom, as a place of shelter, and as what, together with custom, determines character in its various registers; and, finally, ἦθος names the site of discursive dissemination. This range of senses (in the originary sense of *sense*) cannot be reduced to a single overarching unity. There is no concept of ἦθος.

It is only about this one word that, in the voice of the ventriloquist, certain of those who abide nearer the origin have spoken. Thus is voice given to a series of discourses into which this word is inextricably woven and in which it sounds in an originary manner. All that has been added outside these discourses is meant simply to supplement them by circling around the sites where they bring to light the senses of ἦθος.

Note to Chapter 1

The lecture on which this chapter is based was originally presented at a conference at Pennsylvania State University celebrating the work of Dennis Schmidt. The lecture was published in *Epoché* with the title "From Abode to Dissemination" (2017).

2 Luminous Space

A. Fog

The scene is evocative and enticing. It is difficult to avoid being drawn into it. There, on the rocky coast of Maine, a rare view of obscurity is offered. On the landward side of a large cove, there is a clearing right at the edge of the water; on the seaward side of the cove, there is an island and an opening onto the ocean. Standing in the clearing near the water's edge, one feels the almost hypnotic effect as the gentle waves lap onto the shore. Yet, not far out from the shore, the surface of the water and the rocks protruding from it fade away into the early morning fog. Everything beyond is so thoroughly enshrouded that not even a vague outline of the island is visible, much less a view of the opening onto the ocean. As there is a complete absence of vision, only an abstract awareness of them, only a pure positing—or rather, a stretching of imagination beyond the visible—is possible. Beyond the most immediate surroundings, nothing is visible except the fog.

In its manner of appearing, the fog reveals that it differs thoroughly from things such as those it enshrouds. Its appearance is so wondrous that it can provoke doubt as to whether the fog is a thing at all. If it is regarded analytically, yet still concretely, a series of mutually opposed features stands out. The features, which pertain to density, weight, and light, respectively, serve, in turn, to disclose the elemental nature of the fog that distinguishes it from things as such.

Seen from the clearing, the fog appears exceedingly thick; all that can be seen is the impossibility of seeing further; there is utter blockage of vision. Nothing in the distance, the island, for instance, is visible; there is only the depth of the fog and the density with which it veils everything except the most immediate surroundings. And yet, fog is also precisely the opposite: nothing other than air, invisible as it is, is thinner than fog. Even while remaining stationary, one senses that passage through the fog would encounter nothing that would even slightly impede its motion. This utter lack of resistance, which one pictures to oneself, could be confirmed if one were to row out even a short distance into the fog. One would then observe how, as the boat passes through it, the fog dissipates momentarily around the boat as if clearing its way. The fog appears as if it were insubstantial, as if it consisted solely in the obscuring without there being anything solid that would effect the obscuring.

The fog also displays two opposed features with regard to weight. To speak of heavy fog is common parlance, for fog can descend over an area as though it were a weighty mantle spread over it. And yet, it is so light that as it lifts it can float slowly over the surface below or can remain entirely suspended there as if immune to the force of gravity.

The opposed features bearing on the closure of light portend prospects that will prove to advance beyond the mere observation of fog. Fog is closed off from sunlight, and the obscurity that it casts over things consists in the blockage or deprivation of light. This closure is most strikingly revealed when, even if only slightly, even if only momentarily, it is punctured, when there is an opening, that lets the sun break through. And yet, even short of such a breakthrough of light, fog is not itself simply dark but in its very obscuring has its own brightness, its own shining, within—and even beyond—itself. It is as if it could generate light itself, sheltering within itself a spark that could flare up, portending the sunlight that could suddenly break through the obscurity.

There is no such thing as fog. The oppositions inherent in it are not those—if there are any—of things. No things display the phenomenal guise in which fog appears, the spread of its almost insubstantial obscuring. Any dissimulation that it might assume, disguising itself as a property of a thing, would inevitably be betrayed by its indeterminateness. Fog has almost no color; its grayness is little more than simply lack of color. Its extension is so indefinite that it would yield, if at all, only to fractal geometry; to attempt to determine the breadth of its spread would be like trying to measure the perimeter of an irregularly shaped lake, only to discover that the result would vary widely depending on the size of the unit of measure employed.

As morning gives way to afternoon, the sun begins to burn away the fog. It grows thinner and gradually starts to dissipate. The things across from the vantage point, still somewhat enshrouded, slowly become visible, though they remain vague and indistinct. One sees them through the fog, which, though thinner, is still spread throughout the entire area around and above the cove. This configuration is the most consequential: for one sees—if still vaguely—not only the things across the way but also the intervening medium. What previously was attained only by the excessive stretch of imagination begins to offer itself to sense; in its inceptual manifestness it begins to catch up with itself. The medium— the thin fog stretching across the cove—offers a phenomenal figure of the space around the cove; it becomes an adumbration of the space, a visible double of the very space it occupies. In the guise of the fog, the space appears, but not as space, not as itself, but rather only in the shape of the fog. By opening to vision as it thins out, the fog lends visibility to the space, which, as such, is invisible; it renders the invisible visible. In the guise of the fog, the invisible space becomes visible. The fog mediates the opposition between space and visibility, not by dissolving the opposition but by being interposed as a visible surrogate. This scene of substitution offers a phenomenal attestation of the space around the cove and thereby broaches an intimation of space as such.

Yet, such an attestation is not simply an image that, set before one's vision, would reveal an original imaged by it. The fog is not an image of the space it occupies but rather a visible opening upon this space. What happens as the fog begins to rise is a clearing that lets the space become manifest in and through its congruence with the fog.

The scene of attenuating fog will not endure for long. Once the fog lifts, some patches may remain suspended above the cove, as if enticing retention of the disclosure that will have come about. Now one's vision extends without interruption across the entire cove; no obscurity interposes itself between one's vision and all that lies beyond at the far end of the cove. Now one sees clearly not only the island but also the opening onto the ocean. Beyond this opening the water appears to extend without limit. While the phenomenal disclosure effected by the fog warrants a positing of space as such, the gradual clearing that lets the ocean come into view displays the extension of space beyond the cove.

There are not only visible openings onto space but also sonorous clearings in and through which space becomes audible.

The magnificent Gothic cathedral towers above the city of Freiburg. To the east lie the mountains of the upper Black Forest, rising almost vertically at the edge of the city. To the west there stretches the Rhein plain; on a bright, clear day, the river can be seen sparkling in the distance, and, still farther, across the border the contours of the Vosges Mountains can be discerned. Yet, it is around the cathedral, the Freiburger Münster, that the entire expanse is gathered, mountains and plain, the near and the far.

Like most cities going back to the Middle Ages, Freiburg was laid out according to the design by which the cathedral was surrounded by an open space, a kind of ring surrounding the cathedral. On market days it is filled with stalls where farmers and tradesmen sell their goods. Around the periphery are cafes serving the local wines.

When the ancient bells in the tower announce the time of day and, still more, when in late afternoon their tolling continues for quite some time, everything and everyone around the Münster are effectively reduced to silence; even if one speaks, one has little chance of being heard. The vanities of human speech are reduced to naught by the sounding of time's advance. If one hears the bells from farther out in the city, one may gain some sense of the spread of the sound in the open air; then one may awaken to an intimation of the sound's range, of its reach into an indeterminate distance, of the expansiveness of space itself.

From the market square one may on occasion hear faintly the sound of the organ inside the Münster. But everything visible or audible looks or sounds incomparably different once one passes through the elaborate portal and enters the cathedral space. Even the softest tones of the organ surround one completely; one's audition will be drawn completely into the flow of overlapping tones, and a somatic penetration by the sound will be felt.

On certain evenings during the summer months, organ recitals take place in the Münster. Traditional works such as Bach's Toccata and Fugue in D minor as well as music by later composers such as Widor and Reger are performed by distinguished organists. During such performances one cannot resist becoming totally engrossed in the music, though one's aural engagement will be supplemented by the sense of the surroundings: the long nave leading to the altar and, most impressively, the pillars reaching upward to the arches, as if stone, like the soul, could ascend, overcoming its earthy heaviness.

In the Münster there are four organs strategically placed at different locations. Each can be played alone, but they can all be played at the same time from a common console stationed on the platform near the front of the cathedral near the altar. The organs can be played antiphonally side-by-side, front-to-back, or crisscross; or their forces can be united to produce an overwhelming tumult of sound.

The relation of musical sound to its source involves two almost contradictory factors. On the one hand, no advance of the sound from its source can be detected; it has no perceptible forward edge, but rather has always already arrived at the place of the listener, sounding instantaneously from the moment the music begins. On the other hand, despite all the reverberations produced in a huge cathedral, one hears the sound *as* coming from a particular source, or at least from a particular location. The sound is there at once with the auditor, and yet it presents itself as having a definite directionality. When all four organs in the Münster sound at once, the directionalities tend to be leveled out, though even the briefest intervals between the soundings of the various organs leave a degree of directionality intact. Yet, when all four organs play together, the interior of the cathedral is completely filled with sound. Then the sound seems to the listener to be without origin.

The thesis has often been proposed that music is an exclusively temporal art in contrast to such allegedly spatial arts as painting.[1] However, this thesis cannot be sustained: music does not simply fall on the side of the temporal, nor

---

1. "The domain of music is time; that of painting is space." Jean-Jacques Rousseau, *Essay on the Origin of Languages*, trans. J. H. Moran and A. Gode (Chicago: University of Chicago Press, 1966), 62. It is striking that Rousseau maintains such strict separation, considering that he was both a very successful composer and one of the most astute theoreticians of music. Considered in its context, this separation proves to be connected with Rousseau's conception of music as primarily melody and hence with his opposition to the practice of those who, like his rival, Rameau, advocated complex harmony in which within the same time interval distinct tones would be, as it were, stacked up as if spatially related. Thus, immediately following his statement about the respective domains of music and of painting, Rousseau writes: "To multiply the sounds heard at a given time or to present colors in sequence is to alter their economy, putting the eye in the place of the ear and the ear in the place of the eye."

is painting limited to the spatial. Even if the temporality of music is more immediately apparent, music displays multiple forms of spatiality; just as, inversely, painting exhibits temporality, for instance, in its capacity to trace lines of movement. There is perhaps no more decisive demonstration of the spatiality of music than an organ performance in a great cathedral.

For the musical disclosure of space itself within a great cathedral, what is most consequential is the moment when the music has just come to an end but has not yet been superseded by silence. It is within this brief interval, which lasts only a few seconds, that it is possible to hear the space that is enclosed within the interior of the cathedral. In the Freiburger Münster the reverberation time, *die Echozeit*, is six seconds. During this brief temporal interval, the music, though no longer sounding, is sustained as echoes. Thus, during the echo-time the music is still there in the form of echoes. And yet, the music itself is not there; it has come to an end and is no longer sounding. As being both there and not there, the music is in a process of growing quiet, of quieting. Whereas before the music ended, it filled the interior space of the cathedral and its sounding rendered all others virtually inaudible, its quieting exposes a sonorous clearing in which space can be heard. As they reverberate, the echoes offer an audible phenomenon disclosive of the space within the cathedral, a sounding that is an audible double of this space and that thus lets the space be heard in and from its double. Space comes to sound, but not as space, not as itself, but only in the sounding of the echoes. The echoes lend audibility to space, let it sound even though as such it is consigned to silence, is intrinsically silent. The echoes render the inaudible—space as such—audible. By way of the echoes as they sound during the interval of quieting, an intimation of space is broached.

B. Invisible Space

But what is space as such? Most evidently, it is to be distinguished from things: things have properties by which each is defined, whereas space, in whatever way it may be determined, does not possess properties adhering to it itself. In order to formulate appropriately the question, What is space? it is necessary to displace the sense of whatness from that which it has in reference to things. Yet, to do so by reverting from the sense of whatness as universal to that of εἶδος—translated as *look*—does not suffice, for space has no look; it is, as such, invisible. In a certain manner, space is opposed—though not in a merely symmetrical opposition—to the eidetic: whereas it is invisible, the eidetic is precisely that which bestows visibility upon all things. And yet, like the eidetic, it is presupposed by things: as there is no thing that has no look,[2] however minimal its look may be—like hair, mud, and dirt—there are no things that are not in space. It is the nature of all things that

---

2. In declaring that there is nothing that has no look, consideration of certain recent astronomical discoveries, such as that of black holes, is deferred.

they must be in space, on pain of being nothing at all. Space is a precondition of all things, of their being at all. For whatever may cling to being, coming to be and passing away, space is already there. And yet, how can space *be there* unless there is already a *there* in which space is located, another space presupposed by space?

How, then, is a determination of space possible, and how is the vitiating infinite regress to be warded off? How is a way to be found beyond the almost vacuous and quite abstract determination of space as the precondition of all things?

It is possible to advance beyond this aporia only by bringing into play certain phenomena that attest to space, phenomena that are distinct from space by virtue of their phenomenality but that adhere to it in such a manner that they offer an intimation, a proximal intuition, of space. Reflection on space and resolution of the aporia with which the determination of it is burdened must call to its aid certain phenomenal attestations; it must have recourse to such phenomena as the attenuating fog as it lifts from the cove and the echoes of music that fill the space of the cathedral. These phenomena render space visible and audible, not in and of itself, but in these visible and audible doubles, these phenomenal surrogates. However, it is not at all a matter of abandoning the discourse aimed at delimiting space as such; rather, in appealing to these phenomena, the intent is to open the way to a more concrete and determinate discourse.

Yet, certain determinations of space itself can be brought to light almost immediately.

Space is irreducibly singular. It is *one*, unassimilable both to particularity and to universality. In classical terms: "one can represent only one space, and if one speaks of many spaces, one means thereby only parts of one and the same unique space."[3] Space is neither a particular, exemplifying a universal, nor is it itself a universal, for partition is entirely distinct from exemplification. As regards space, exemplarity has no pertinence whatsoever.

As parts of "one and the same unique space," spaces are distinguished by their limitedness. In a classical formulation: "Space is essentially one; the manifold in it, and thus the general concept of spaces, depends solely on limitations."[4] As the basis of all limitation by which spaces are determined, space is not itself determined by limitation; that is, it is unlimited. Though it can sustain limitations

---

3. Kant, *Kritik der reinen Vernunft*, A25/B39.

4. Ibid. In this passage Kant's reference to "the general concept of spaces" cannot consistently be taken to construe either space or the manifold of spaces as conceptual. Indeed in the very next sentence he declares that space—and consequently the spaces that partition it—is an *a priori* intuition, which "underlies all concepts of space"; it is from space as intuition that all concepts of space are abstracted. Space is, first of all, intuition, and any concepts of it that may be formed are strictly secondary. In the present context, Kant employs *concept* to designate *determination*, namely, that all spaces are determined by limitation, that is, as limited, in contrast to the unlimitedness of space as such.

that are such as to delimit spaces within it, it cannot itself, *as itself*, undergo limitation, since this would violate its essential oneness. Absolved of limitation, space itself is unlimited.

Yet, just as spaces extend in space within limits, so it would seem that space itself, presumably extending without limit, would require another space within which it would be extended. Again the aporia appears: there seems to be no way by which to avoid falling into an infinite regress. However, the unlimitedness of space does not consist merely in its running on and on. Space does not primarily extend in a linear manner. It is not as if it were like a line drawn continuously and interminably on a flat sheet of paper laid out in advance without end. It is, rather, as if there were a roll of paper that unrolled precisely as the line was being drawn and by means of the process of drawing. That in which space extends does not preexist the extending but rather unfolds in and through the extending and indeed is nothing other than the space that is extending. Space itself, in extending, generates the very space in which it extends and is identical with that space. It is a matter not just of unlimited spatial extension but of originary spacing, that is, of an event in which space itself, as it extends itself without limit, opens the very space of its own extending, coalescing entirely with it. In other words, space spaces itself. As spacing, space relates to itself, as if, in a unique sense, it were curved, as if, again in a unique sense, it were absolute.

It is as spacing that the unlimitedness of space has its most originary sense. In turn, spacing originates the extension of space as linearly unlimited, that is, it founds spatial extension in the more common sense. It is primarily spacing in this founded mode that can be glimpsed through phenomenal attestations, though not without tacit reference to spacing as such.

Once the fog has begun to lift, lending visibility to space, it gradually clears away so that one's view across the cove extends to the distant opening onto the ocean. This visible protraction out to the ocean, which appears as extending on without any visible limit, composes a figure, a visible double, of unlimitedly extending space. The advance of one's vision as the fog clears away attests, if more remotely, to the progressive self-unfolding of space; it attests to spacing as such.

If one walks rapidly westward through the city as the prolonged tolling of the bells of the Münster continues, the intensity of the sound will gradually diminish. One is naturally aware that there are places farther west—most certainly in the Vosges Mountains across the Rhein in France—where the bells will not be heard. But what is remarkable is that it is not possible to determine a precise point, a distance, where the sound of the bells can no longer be heard, partly because of the variation in the volume of the tolling, but also, more significantly, because of the indeterminateness of the distance. This indeterminateness offers an audible double of the indeterminateness of space itself. Yet, to be indeterminate is to have no determinable limit and in this sense to be unlimited.

The same phenomenal figure occurs in relation to the sound of the organs. If one leaves the cathedral while the organs are being played, one will continue to hear them as one walks across the square outside the cathedral, though the sound will be softer. If from the square one walks westward through the city, one will not be able to determine a precise point at which the sound of the organs can no longer be heard. The extension of the sounding is indeterminate, no less than that of the bells. The indetermination of the auditory limit is the audible counterpart of the unlimitedness of space, for to be indeterminate is to be without a determinable limit. Because the extension of the sound is, at its limit, without limit, it doubles the unlimitedness of space. Its capacity to attest to the unlimitedness of space is the result of its indeterminate, unlimited, limit.

Both in the case of the cove and the opening of the vista beyond to the ocean and in that of the cathedral and the distancing from it, phenomenal doubles of space and its unlimited extension are produced. Such doubling has, in turn, a double structure: the visible or audible counterpart exposes the space, which, at once, withdraws from exposure, maintaining its difference from its phenomenal figure. Thus, this figure is both congruent with the space it reveals and yet distinct from it. Whereas the figure is fully present (or, more precisely, horizonally present) to visual or auditory apprehension, space itself remains withdrawn from direct presence despite being sensibly figured. It offers, as it were, only a shadow of itself, while remaining itself detached from presence. And yet, space is everywhere;[5] it is the very condition for every "where." There is nowhere where space is not; or rather, it is the very condition for presence. It is only within invisible, inaudible space that things can become present so as to present themselves to vision and audition.

By discerning and drawing out certain implications broached in the transition between space and spaces, between unlimited and limited, it is possible to formulate a series of determinations of space as such.[6] In each connection such transitional thinking will be supplemented by appeal to phenomenal attestations, such as those displayed within the cove and within the cathedral.

---

5. "One can never form a representation that there is no space, though one can quite well think that no objects are to be found in it" (ibid., A24/B38).
6. In these formulations three words will be used that are virtually synonymous: *delimit*, *define*, and *determine*. All three words mean *to limit*; in the present context, each has as its specific meaning, respectively: to establish a limit, to mark the limit of something, to circumscribe something by identifying its limits. They can also refer, if more indirectly, to the process in which limitation comes about in relation to the unlimited. The three words are etymologically different, deriving, respectively, from *limes* (ὅρος), *finis*, and *terminus*, though these roots converge toward a single meaning.

   In referring to the *determination* of space, it is of utmost importance to twist this word away from the common meaning, which *delimitation* and *defining* or *definition* will retain. A determination of space cannot be a marking of limits, for space is, by its very nature, unlimited. The appropriate strategy is to release *determination* into a sphere of neutrality in order, then, to let its meaning (in the present context) emerge from the formulations of the determinations of space.

In order to delimit the first (already broached) determination, there is required only a direct phenomenal observation issuing into passage between visible and invisible, audible and inaudible. One cannot see space, nor can one even imagine what it would be to see space. One sees only things in space; even if, for instance, one envisions pure mathematical figures not visible to sensible vision, it is only the figures that one sees, as it were, in the mind's eye, never the space in which these figures are seen. Space—even if imaginary—cannot be seen: it is intrinsically, by its very nature, invisible. One does not see the space attested by the attenuating fog but only the fog as it doubles the space around and above the cove.

Space is also inaudible. In the cathedral one hears the echoes, not the space to which they attest. What differentiates inaudibility from invisibility is the fact that most things do not themselves emit sounds (though they can of course be made to emit sounds by the application of force or the effect of the wind). They cannot, then, be themselves heard, just as the space in which they are situated cannot as such be heard. Whereas things in space are visible, these things are, for the most part, inaudible. The strict difference between space as invisible and things as visible is blurred in the case of audition.

The second determination of space moves between limited and unlimited: in and of itself space possesses no shape or form, for these require definite outlines, defining limits, whereas space as such is unlimited. Although shapes or forms can be brought to bear on space, their imposition would consist precisely in introducing limits into space, thereby constituting spaces, and thus effecting a transition from space to spaces. These spaces can display shapes or forms by way of the things harbored within them, but space as such will remain unlimited, immune to delimitation. In other words, there can be no geometry of space as such.

Though by their very nature, phenomena cannot be unlimited, there are phenomena that can, within limits, attest that space as such is shapeless and formless. As fog begins to lift from the cove, it floats freely and constantly changes its shape, almost as if it had no shape at all. Almost as light and thin as air, it continually drifts without ever quite assuming a definite form, approximating as closely as possible a condition of shapelessness and formlessness.

The third determination is set at the point where things and forms pass into space. This determination has a double import: space as such is all-encompassing and all-receiving. As all-encompassing it grants place for all things. Things are situated in various spaces where each has its place. Yet spaces are constituted by limitation that comes to bear on unlimited space as such, and thus all spaces belong within unlimited space, as do, consequently, all the things situated in these spaces. All things are in space, that is, space is all-encompassing. By completely filling the cove such that initially almost nothing escapes its obscuring effect, the fog attests that space is all-encompassing; as do the echoes as they completely fill the interior of the cathedral.

Space is all-receiving. It is receptive to every form that, having gained a certain—though never total—independence, approaches it. Because space has no form, it is completely promiscuous. It offers no resistance to any forms that might come to enter it; since it is entirely lacking in form, no form that enters it is opposed to it, and thus none are to be repulsed. It is like a block of wax, which can be imprinted with any and every shape and form. It is like the fog, which captures all things in its obscurity.

The fourth determination is set at two closely allied points of defense: space is ever-enduring, for there is nothing that could destroy it. Since it is, as such, unlimited, there can be no division within it—no positing of limits—by which opposed, hence destructive, segments could arise. Even if somehow a force-bearing, destructive moment that had gained a certain independence should assault space from without, the invisibility of space would give it an unlimited capacity to elude this assaulting force. Even if elusion should fail—and it could not—space as all-receiving would simply receive the would-be destroyer while offering nothing that could be destroyed. It is as if a figure were to be stamped onto a block of wax, set into the wax, set into it with destructive intent; the wax would simply receive the imprint and eventually, when the wax came to be remodeled, reshaped, the imprint would be effaced and the wax into which it had been set would be remolded into the block as a whole.

The fact that an assault from without that would have to be eluded is impossible and that there is no outside but only limitation shows all the more decisively that space is ever-enduring. It is indeed unthinkable that space could cease to be. The very sense of cessation pertains only to that of things in space; if space ceased to be, there could be no cessation—that is, space cannot, by its very nature, cease to be.

All morning long the fog endures, obscuring virtually the entire cove as well as the island and the opening onto the ocean that lie beyond it. Throughout this entire time nothing in particular can be distinguished from anything else. The fog remains a thick, heavy cover and is neither penetrated nor dissipated by the sunlight. Though the duration of their sounding is much briefer, the echoes that fill the cathedral represent the way in which, after it has ended, the music endures.

The final determination proceeds from the initial determination of space as invisible and inaudible; it also bears a certain reference back to all the previous determinations. It traces the movement of thought between space and spaces.

Space is not given to sense. It is not aesthetic but rather noetic. This is the final determination: space is noetic, is accessible only to thought. Insofar as thought is oriented to space and everything allied with space, thinking assumes a specific guise and is structured in a definitive way: to think is to delimit; it is to discern and display the defining limits of that which is to be thought. The display of limits can be carried out in multiple ways, not only by abstracting concepts but also by drafting schemata. Yet, space as such is unlimited; there are no limits to be discerned and displayed—that is, space intrinsically resists thought, withholds itself from every effort to submit it to thought. Limits arise only when space is articulated into delimited spaces, though such articulation leaves space as such unaffected, no less unlimited. It is like a block of wax that, though cut into discrete pieces, retains the same composition as prior to the scission. If space as such is to be thought, this thinking must attend either to the moment when spaces, and therefore limits, arise from— that is, by limitation of—space as such; or, correlatively, to the moment when, from the spaces, and therefore the limits, that have just arisen, space as such withdraws from limitation. Thought can—as in the formulation of these determinations— get a glimpse of space as such only in these moments of transition—which is to say that it is most difficult to catch. The effort required is an intensification of that in which one would attempt to discern the moment when the amorphous spread of the fog congeals into a shape capable of attesting to the space within the cove. Much the same effort would be required in order to discern the moment when the articulated music passes over into the more or less uniform echoes.

Let us return to the scene of the cove. There, in the small clearing, others may share the view. Stationed at this secluded spot on the coast of Maine, feeling the cool breeze coming from the sea, smelling the salty air, listening to the gentle waves as they wash over the rocks, peering into the fog, anticipating that it will lift and that eventually the sun will break through—each of those present is immersed in these concrete particularities; they are absorbed in their own sensuous experience: they are not ideal subjects but embodied singularities. Their reversion, their turn back into their own self, is mediated by all that is offered to their senses, by reflection back not only from the visible but also from what is heard, smelled, felt. Yet, at this site it is vision that is predominant, for they are drawn out of themselves by the view across the cove.

These singular beings are thus ecstatic in their way of being. This being is said in many ways. Each is a being that is bound to itself, a self that, from birth, is none other than itself. Each is a being that unaccountably finds itself there where it is, unable to recall the natal event by which it came to be; it is a being subject to natality. Each is a being, an animal, that speaks as no other animal can except in the most rudimentary way. Its title, ζῷον λόγον ἔχον, passes into *animal rationale*; it comes to be called the *rational animal*, the animal having reason. This being is a *person*, one who is free yet bound by moral laws. It is the living being that is capable of death, a *mortal*. It is the being that is bound to the earth (*humus*) and can accordingly be called *human* (*homō*).[7] All these are truthful—that

---

7. "*Human* comes via Old French *humain* from Latin *hūmānus*. Like *homō* (*human being*), this was related to Latin *humus* (*earth*) and was used originally for 'people' in the sense 'earthly beings' (in contrast with the immortal gods)." John Ayto, *Dictionary of Word Origins* (New York: Arcade Publishing, 2011), s.v. "human." The connection between *homō* and *humus* is also affirmed in *Webster's New Twentieth Century Dictionary*, 2nd ed. (Cleveland: World Publishing, 1970), s.v. "human."

is, disclosive—ways of saying what this being is, and each name is inscribed in various discourses that not only explicate what is said in the name but also demonstrate that it draws out a determining trait of this being. Within the broad context in which preeminence is accorded to the concrete engagement of this being with natural elements and paradigmatically to its attachment to the earth as a principal trait, it is most appropriately designated as *human*. Within the more specific context in which this being is regarded as bound by ethicality and as capable, therefore, of sustaining itself in its dignity, its most proper name is *person*.

It is the engagement with nature and the natural elements that enables humans to apprehend phenomena that attest to space as such, phenomena such as the attenuating fog. Such attestation can also be found in other locations. On the Greek island of Naxos, gazing out across the Aegean, one may be entranced as the sun rises from the sea and casts its brilliant panoply, its rosy fingers, up into the sky. As the rising sun's rays extend into the sky, an intimation of space, indeed of the illumination of space, may be granted. In the Dolomites in northern Italy, one may be unnerved at the sight of a sudden bolt of lightning splitting the sky above the peaks of the mountains and at the sound of the thunder as it echoes from the mountains and outlines the space around the mountain range. In the case both of the sunrise and of the lightning, the sky is as evocative as the earth—perhaps even more so—and accordingly may prompt an intimation of space as such. Thunder can do so even more directly, as its sound reverberates across the space of the deep mountain valleys. The fact that in these occurrences earth and sky are bound together, if in very different ways, demonstrates that to be attached to the earth is also to be attentive to the sky. To call this being by the name *human* is to indicate most directly that its native realm is the space delimited by earth and sky.

C. The Time and Place of Light

Space is not to be seen. It cannot be seen. There is no vision to which it can become manifest. It is unconditionally, inviolably invisible. If ever there is to be visibility, light must enter space and spread across the expanse in which visibility will become possible. It must bring to bear its capacity as the "force of filling space."[8] These happenings, the entry of light into space, its spread across space, and its filling of space, are lacking in determinacy as a result of the indeterminacy, the unlimitedness, of space as such, of its lack of the bounds and articulation that it will acquire only in the progression to the elements and beyond.

And yet, like space, light as such is completely invisible. It can gain a certain apparent—though derivative—visibility only if it illuminates something, only if it lets something come to light and thereby become manifest; but even in this case

---

8. G. W. F. Hegel, *Enzyklopädie der philosophischen Wissenschaften*, Zweiter Teil (Frankfurt a.M.: Suhrkamp, 1970), §275 *Zusatz*.

it is that which is illuminated, absorbing and reflecting the light, that is seen, not the light itself. Even when, for example, particles of dust in the air make it possible to discern a beam of light, one sees only a band of illuminated dust, not the light itself.[9] In Hegel's formulation: light is a "pure making manifest [*Manifestieren*] that is nothing but a *making manifest*."[10]

Light brings radiance. Its entry into space and its spread therein renders space luminous. It is only in luminous space that self-showing can occur, that something can become manifest. It is not that prior to the spread of light that which subsequently comes to be manifest will have been entirely hidden, will have lain under a blanket of darkness. On the contrary, it will have been neither manifest nor hidden, for it is only within luminous space that the alternatives of light and dark, manifest and concealed, are first constituted as such. Only when—in a time before time—light streams into space does it become possible for anything to show itself, to become visible; this condition holds even in cases in which something shows itself as concealed, betraying its concealment through a privative self-showing. What is most remarkable is that the very conditions of visibility, namely, space and light, are themselves invisible; it is the invisible that enables the visible. All that is visible, all that manifestly shows itself, even that which shows itself by withdrawing from self-showing, can visibly appear only within the scope of the invisible. Yet, this appearing does not render the invisible visible; no matter what may show itself within luminous space, both space and light remain invisible. The spread of light throughout measureless space induces the radiance of all things, yet it shares not the least in this radiance. Luminous space remains unconditionally withdrawn from visibility.

Space as such, even if filled with light, cannot be seen, and a true discourse, one disclosive of luminous space, cannot take the form of a transcription of a vision, for space, because it is invisible, displays no look that could be transposed into script. Neither does light display a look, even though it renders possible all shinings of looks. A true discourse on luminous space can proceed only by

---

9. In scientific practice light can be registered on an appropriate apparatus, even on a simple light meter. Its invariant velocity is determinable and, in turn, determines the temporal interval between the occurrence of an astral event and its reception by an earthly observer. Yet in none of these connections does light itself become visible but only its effect on or conveyance of something distinct from it. Light is no more visible than any other form on the electromagnetic spectrum (such as radio waves), and yet it is distinctive by virtue of its capacity to make visible.

10. Hegel, *Enzyklopädie*, Zweiter Teil, §276. An artistic affirmation of the pure transparency of light, of its invisibility and consequent immateriality, is found in Frank Lloyd Wright's insight into the relation between light and glass. He once described glass as "the materialization of light, the weightless medium of sight." Donald Hoffmann, *Frank Lloyd Wright: Architecture and Nature* (New York: Dover Publications, 1986), 29. His unique way of using glass in his architectural structures served to diminish the visual barrier between inside and outside; the glass allowed light to flood into a building in an unprecedented manner.

discerning and making explicit the progression from space to things in their self-showing. This progression can, in turn, be supplemented and concretized by expressing phenomena that—like the fog, the echoes, the dawn, the storm—attest to luminous space but also, less directly, to the progression from luminous space.

The intractable invisibility of light is attested by the fact that even the light of the sun, of the primary source of light, eludes vision. If one glances at the sun, the brilliance of its shining will prove to be so intense that the shining of its light and the appearance of the sun coalesce, and it may seem, then, that in seeing the sun in its brilliance, one gets a view of light at its very source. And yet, even if it were granted that to see the sun is to see light, which in this case would prove to be visible at its source, the decisive question is whether (and if so, to what extent) vision of the sun is possible. This is precisely the possibility that Socrates put in question. In the warning that he gave to himself, he expressed his fear that he would be blinded if he looked directly at the sun. Even if, as he observed, one looks at it during an eclipse, this danger remains; indeed, in this case one is more exposed to the fate of blindness, since, as is common knowledge, it is during an eclipse that one can most easily sustain looking at the sun and thereby incur the greatest danger. In attempting to get a view of the sun itself, one would end up being deprived of all access to the visible; and since this failed attempt would have been ventured precisely during an eclipse, during a time when the sun is completely obscured, one would not—before blindness set in—actually see the sun at all. If at other times one attempts to look at the sun, only a momentary glance can be endured; it is as if the sun withdrew from whatever minimal visibility it might have allowed during that moment. Socrates prescribed that the only safe way to look at the sun is to look at its reflection in water or in some other such thing; but then one will be looking neither at the sun nor at the light itself but rather at something—a reflection—formed by the light striking—that is, illuminating in a certain way—the water or some other such thing. Even as one sees a reflection of the sun, the light itself will remain invisible.[11]

Yet, the light of the sun alternates with its privation. Even in the night, one may imagine the sun casting its light elsewhere, perhaps along some mythically represented course, perhaps as represented in modern scientific terms. Even the privation of the sun's light is—except in the most exceptional cases—no mere privation, no abject negativity replacing the pure solar phenomenon. Night is, rather, like a shadow that accompanies light; it is like the shadow cast by a small conifer illuminated obliquely from the other side. Nightfall is an event not unlike that of stepping back into the conifer's shadow, or of retreating into the shade of an olive tree bathed in the brilliant light of a Greek landscape.

---

11. See Plato, *Phaedo* 99d–e; also my discussion in *The Figure of Nature: On Greek Origins* (Bloomington: Indiana University Press, 2016), 227–41.

As the sun follows its course across the sky, there are various points that it crosses and certain differentiated segments that it traverses: dawn, sunrise, morning, noon, afternoon, sunset, dusk. In this way the sun's movement along its itinerary provides the original natural clock; in this movement, time is made visible. It is from the sky that time shows itself.[12] It is not that time is anterior to the sky and to the movement of the sun (which is *of* the sky) across it; it is not as though time already somehow *is* (the *already* implying a time before time) and then comes to have the celestial sphere as the locus of its appearance. Neither is the sky—nor other natural elements—somehow anterior to time (here again a time before time is implied), providing, in advance, a place where time could come to appear. Rather, the sky with its itinerant sun is interlaced with time. It is a matter not of anteriority at all but rather of interlacement.[13]

Yet, in addition to the movement of the sun, there are other progressions or circulations that, though mundane, have the capacity to render time visible at least across a certain span: the change that most natural things undergo in the course of the seasons; the annual recurrence of the seasons; and the maturation and aging of living beings. However, these movements are all, in certain respects, governed by solar movement. The course of the seasons follows the variation in the elevation that the sun's daily course has above the horizon; this variation produces change in the conditions to which living beings are exposed and hence change in these beings themselves. The recurrence of the seasons corresponds to the sun's annual repetition of its movement between the summer solstice and the winter solstice. This repetition defines the year, which provides the measure of age. Thus, the sun's solstitial movement is instrumental in rendering visible the more extended periods of time, as the sun's movement across the sky from dawn to dusk renders visible the day and the time of day. And yet, as noted, the moon and even the stars can—and in some cultures do—provide the reference by which to measure time.[14] The rotation of the starry heaven is perhaps most capable of making visible the circularity belonging to time.

---

12. Not all cultures measure time by reference to the sun and design calendars accordingly. In contrast to the solar-based Gregorian calendar used in the West, the Islamic calendar (*Hijri*) used a pure lunar system. Time is measured by reference to the phases of the moon; the system is completely independent of the solar cycle. Another system is represented by the traditional Hebrew calendar, which combines lunar and solar references: its months are lunar, but its years are solar. Still another system is that of the Inuit, an indigenous people living in northern Canada and Alaska. They reckon time by neither the sun nor the moon but by the stars. For instance, the appearance of stars in Orion's shoulder is the mark of winter. It is significant that in all these instances the measure of time derives from the movement of heavenly bodies, that is, from the sky.

13. See my extended analysis in *Force of Imagination: The Sense of the Elemental* (Bloomington: Indiana University Press, 2000), 184–92.

14. See note 12.

The movements of the sun, the moon, and the stars constitute what was once described as the moving image of perpetuity and as inseparable from time itself.

The sun's daily course measures out both the sunlit day and its privation, the night with its veil of darkness. Yet, night is not just the symmetrical opposite of day but an opposite that houses its opposite, that in this sense is opposed to itself precisely in being itself. Night is not solely night but also harbors the promise of the coming day. This promise is displayed, made visible in the blackness of the night, by the nocturnal spectacle of light: the moon and the stars. Were the night to promise no arrival of day, were it a total, uncompromising denial of any coming dawn, of light that would dispel the night, then it would be nothing short of absolute night, the primary name of which is death—both as such and in its manifold semantic and metaphorical displacements. There is perhaps no question that swings more undecidably between the two alternatives: whether unbounded anxiety is the only possibility as one is confronted by the threat of utter extinction, by the certainty of the coming darkness; or whether the tranquil repose most beautifully presented in the Platonic portrayal of Socrates's death remains an open possibility.

Space admits not only light but also air. Just as light brings visibility, so air opens space to audibility, to sounding, and, above all, to the sounding of speech. It was, most likely, because of this gift that Anaximenes reportedly declared: "I praise and honor air."[15] Like space and light, air as such is invisible: one sees things that sound or persons that speak, but one does not see the intervening air, though it conveys the sound, just as light offers the look of things. Air as such is also inaudible. One hears the howling wind sweeping across the land in a winter storm, and one listens to the rustling of leaves occasioned by a gentle summer breeze. But what one hears is not air as such but only as it is given voice by the contours of the landscape or by the array of foliage. Inaudible air is what makes audibility and hence audition possible. As the invisible enables visibility, so the inaudible enables audibility.[16]

Even as receptive of light and air, space does not suffice for the self-showing of things. For it is only an indefinite expanse, a mere there. Its luminosity adds only the possibility of visibility, just as the air that comes to fill it brings only the

---

15. Daniel W. Graham, ed. and trans., *The Texts of Early Greek Philosophy* (Cambridge: Cambridge University Press, 2010), pt. 1, p. 85.
16. There are certain ways in which the relation between air and audibility differs from that between light and visibility. There are media other than air, for example, water, that can convey sound and thereby render certain things audible; whereas only light can render things visible (except in very exceptional cases where other forms of electromagnetic radiation such as X-rays are used). Furthermore, audition is less capable of revealing things than is vision, though audition of human speech can reveal, though in a different direction, traits of the speaker and implications of speech (most notably, signification) that are not accessible to vision.

possibility of sounding. Space—even as supplemented by light and air—is form-less: it is completely lacking in measure and bounds, which are necessary if there are to be places in which things can show themselves. It is also completely lack-ing in articulation and differentiation by which things as well as the moments of their self-showing could be distinguished. What is thus required is determina-tion of luminous space in the sense of boundary or limit (*determinatio*), or, more specifically, a series of determinations of luminous space leading to the point where an event of manifestation becomes possible.

There is a story—all too often literalized—according to which all determina-tion originates from a source that is apart from the things that thereby come to be determined. The story—expressed in a language necessarily illegitimate—tells of a threshold: there is the *source* of determination, which lies apart from the *things determined*, and *space*, which grants to things the possibility of being at all, since whatever is a mere thing must be somewhere and, since it *is*, is capable of showing itself with the determination bestowed on it by the source. And yet, this discourse cannot be sustained; it is illegitimate and precisely for this reason is a story. What disrupts it is that to be *apart*, as the source is posited to be, is itself a spatial deter-mination. As the alleged detachment of the source is thwarted, it cannot but prove to fall within luminous space, in which those very things it would determine are situated. But then, it ceases to be the source and becomes, instead, an operation of determination within luminous space. As such it institutes and coalesces with the emergence of a series of determinations of luminous space that, in the end, make it possible for things to show themselves in their determinateness.[17]

In each case the emergence occurs as a positing of limits within luminous space. This positing cannot be a bestowal from a beyond, from outside luminous space, since any beyond or outside would, as itself spatial, be assimilated to lu-minous space. The positing must be effected from within luminous space. It is possible to thematize the limits thus posited, though the positing as such can, it seems, be disclosed only to the extent that it originates from an intrinsic exigency for the limits, the determinations, that are posited. Any further disclosure of the positing of limits may itself be limited, and full transparency is perhaps simply not to be achieved.

The series of determinations is bidirectional. If it is taken to begin with lu-minous space and to proceed through the determinations leading to the mani-festation of things, then its course is that of emergence. If the manifestation of things is taken as the beginning, then the track is that of a regress to conditions of possibility. Because a concrete intimation of space as such has been taken as

---

17. These determinations are different in kind from those previously enumerated. They are not determinations of space as such but of luminous space; they also have a certain orientation to the domain of the manifestation of things, even though they do not yet extend to this domain.

the beginning, the following discourse will trace the course of emergence. But it would also be possible—for instance, beginning with a phenomenological analysis of manifestation—to trace the regress to conditions of possibility.

The first determination of luminous space is constituted by earth and sky. These limit the indefinite expanse of space as such by establishing bounds, by being themselves the upper and lower bounds, which delimit a region, a relatively determinate space, a bounded interspace. Within this space, differentiation is introduced, if only minimally: there is the upper, corresponding to the sky, and the lower, corresponding to the earth; and these bounds define, in turn, the two principal directionalities, that of ascent and that of descent.

While these directionalities and indeed all that is installed within the interspace of earth and sky engender and shape human concerns of numerous sorts and to that extent can be designated as constituting the native realm of humans, it is only through further determinations that the human condition as such takes shape in its manifold dimensions.

It is through its bond to its first determination that luminous space is temporalized. Already in the present discourse it has been shown how time becomes manifest from the sky, preeminently from the movement of the sun. Yet, the relation between time and the sky is not a matter of one being anterior to the other (in any sense—if there be any). The term has already been broached: their relation is, rather, one of interlacement. With the advent (this word must also be crossed out) of the first determination of luminous space, time comes on the scene.

The interspace bounded by earth and sky is anything but a mere homogeneous continuum. Within it there are beings that in various ways indicate or disclose the bounds. Extending from their earthbound roots to their light-seeking crowns, trees represent, on their own scale yet indicatively, the space of earth and sky. There are also animals, especially birds, whose natural movements take the form of gestures toward the sky.

Thoreau had a keen sense for such gestures and recorded in his journals occasions when the span between earth and sky was revealed in this manner. On one occasion the site was Walden, where he was testing whether the water was, as he surmised, cooler than the sand underneath. At 2 p.m. on July 17, 1860, he described this scene and then continued: "The nighthawk's ripping sound, heard overhead these days, reminds us that the sky is, as it were, a roof, and that our world is limited on that side, it being reflected as from a roof back to earth. It does not suggest an infinite depth in the sky, but a nearness to the earth, as of a low roof echoing back its sounds."[18] In these words Thoreau attests that the bird's sound spans the space delimited by sky and earth, that it is like an almost momentary echo from

18. Henry David Thoreau, *The Journal of Henry D. Thoreau*, ed. B. Torrey and F. H. Allen (Boston: Houghton Mifflin, 1949), 13:406–7.

the roof to the ground, from sky to earth. He observes that the resounding does not suggest the infinite distance of the sky but rather displays its nearness to the earth. This serves to emphasize that what is revealed is the space of sky and earth, the space bounded above and below by the sky and the earth.

There are also perfectly still natural settings in which reflections join, precisely in their difference, earth and sky—as in scenes in which configurations of clouds are reflected in the smooth surface of a lake. Mountains, too, have such indicative power: they are of the earth and yet are ascensional, clouds often gathering around their peaks as if drawing the sky downward toward them.

Clouds can also texture the sky, interrupting the pure blue that it as such displays in daylight, patterning the sky with various shapes corresponding to the quality of their shining and their degree of transparency or opaqueness. Textures of numerous sorts belong—indeed in a variety of ways—not only to earth and sky but to all elements of nature.[19]

The second primary determination of luminous space is that by which other natural elementals emerge in the interspace bounded by earth and sky. Some elementals are of brief duration (lightning), some can be measured by minutes or hours (rain), while others persist across a time span so enormous that it requires a special measure (the geological time of a mountain range). There are other elementals that are primarily temporal, though they also infuse the interspace (the day). There are elementals that mediate between earth and sky by means of shadowing, as when the shadows of clouds are cast across a landscape; and there is mediation, as when the reflection of a high, tree-covered mountain appears on the surface of a lake adjacent to it. There are elementals that come from above down to the surface of the earth (rain, snow). There are confluences of elementals (a thunderstorm).

Some elementals define specific regions and corresponding directionalities within the interspace between earth and sky. The Ancients posited natural proclivities that drew the elements to certain regions to such an extent that the identity of the region and of its directionality was defined by the element that naturally belonged there. When Aristotle declares that *up* is "where fire and what is light are carried, and likewise down . . . is where things having heaviness and earthen things are,"[20] he is reiterating Empedocles's words of instruction to Pausanias: that each element honorably guards its abode. To be sure, the topography of the elemental directionalities will prove to be more complex than Empedocles and Aristotle expressly foresaw; while there is indeed layering of elementals, there are also crossovers, intersections, and confluences among the elementals—rethought, as now required, in such a way that they exceed in number and differ

---

19. See my extended analysis of the elementals and their textures in *Logic of Imagination: The Expanse of the Elemental* (Bloomington: Indiana University Press, 2012), 146–53.
20. Aristotle, *Physics* 208b20–22.

in nature from those identified by Aristotle. If, still further, modern cosmology has to a large degree limited and relativized this topography, these age-old directionalities, both as such and as multiply metaphorized, continue to orient the lives of humans: whatever is situated above and draws our vision upward possesses a nobility in contrast to the mundanity of what lies below on the surface of the earth. There is no limit to the ways in which artists can represent the condition of humans as situated between the superior upper region and the earthly, mundane region below and as longing to ascend to the upper region, to free themselves from their earthbound state. Klee's celebrated lithograph *Tightrope Walker* displays this condition: from on high the tightrope walker strives to maintain his position above the ground, though with each step he exposes himself to the danger of losing his balance and falling to the ground at the risk of death. There is also a drawing by Klee entitled *Hardly Still Walking, Not Yet Flying*. It pictures a human figure who is adapted to precisely what the title says: the figure has wings but is not flying; also it has feet and appears to be walking, and yet no ground on which he could walk is shown in the drawing.[21]

At the very beginning of *The Human Condition*, Arendt reflects on the significance of the launch of the first man-made satellite in 1957. She observes that during the "time it managed to stay in the skies, it dwelt and moved in the proximity of the heavenly bodies as though it had been admitted tentatively to their sublime company"; and she declares that this event was "second in importance to no other, not even to the splitting of the atom." She explains that its enormous significance lay in the fact that it was "the first 'step toward escape from man's imprisonment to the earth.'" She concludes with a citation associated with a great Russian scientist: "Mankind will not remain bound to the earth forever." Then, over against this reflection, she asks whether the modern age will "end with an even more fateful repudiation of an Earth who was the Mother of all living creatures under the sky." And then, as if to counter such repudiation, she writes: "The earth is the very quintessence of the human condition."[22]

Elementals not only introduce directionalities into the interspace between earth and sky but also install in this space articulation and differentiation, which, in turn, are precursors of measure. These articulations and differentiations, engendered by elementals and bordering on measure, constitute the third of the determinations of luminous space.

A mountain range marks an articulation and thereby differentiates between the areas on opposite sides of the mountains. The spaces between the various

---

21. Images of these two works are displayed in *Paul Klee: Philosophical Vision; From Nature to Art*, ed. John Sallis (Boston: McMullen Museum of Art, Boston College, 2012), 213, 218. See my discussion of the two works in *Klee's Mirror* (Albany: State University of New York Press, 2015), 4, 73–75.
22. Hannah Arendt, *The Human Condition* (Chicago: University of Chicago Press, 1958), 1–2.

mountains may also function as articulations; moreover the mountains display the difference between upper and lower, locating them at different levels of the earthy protrusion, which constitutes an upsurge of earth toward the sky. Clouds articulate the blue dome of the sky, and, in conjunction with the rain they bring on, they mark corresponding, if indefinite, areas on the earth. A paradigm of articulation is provided by coastlines, which connect, but also separate, land and sea. It is likewise with the differentiation between the day and the night except that the line of the articulation is broadened by the mediation provided by dawn, on the one side, and dusk, on the other.

Furthermore, there is articulation in the diurnal sky between different times of day, and time as such is so inseparable from these articulations that one could say, with only minimal hyperbole, that time is the articulation of the sky. In Monet's series paintings, the times of the day and the times of the year (the seasons) are artistically presented. In the *Wheatstacks* series, in particular, the wheatstack is not the theme of the paintings but only a fulcrum or a reflecting and shadowing shape on which and around which the light, which is the actual theme, is gathered. In these works time is painted by means of the representation of light and air—that is, the atmospheric spread of light—as, at various times of day and of the year, they fill the space of the painting. In the series *Morning on the Seine*, the theme is likewise light and air as they spread into the scene depicted. In this case time is represented as the progression of the day from dawn to morning, the water serving as the fulcrum for the dispersal of the atmosphere-born light.[23]

In contrast to these elemental articulations of earth, sky, and light, there are other natural scenes that under certain conditions display virtually no articulation, though under different conditions quite another pattern may prevail. The surface of the ocean can appear calm and almost mirror-like without any conspicuous waves patterning the surface. A storm disrupts this smooth uniformity, transforming the surface into a scene of interruptive surges; under such conditions there is articulation but of a different kind, articulation that is constantly changing, one wave dispelling another from moment to moment. Rivers are otherwise: as a rule they flow smoothly through their fixed channel thereby providing articulation that separates the two banks. In the case of landscapes, human as well as natural factors are often involved; articulation can be affected by lines of trees, by hills and mountains, or by roads or paths that cut across the landscape.[24]

---

23. See my discussion of the *Wheatstacks* paintings in *Shades—Of Painting at the Limit* (Bloomington: Indiana University Press, 1998), chap. 1. Images of several of the paintings are included. On the *Morning on the Seine* series, see Paul Hayes Tucker, *Monet in the 90s: The Series Paintings* (Boston: Museum of Fine Arts, 1989), chap. 8.
24. Articulations of landscape are represented in an exemplary fashion in Cézanne's paintings of Mont Sainte-Victoire.

Place is the fourth of the determinations of luminous space. It is the result of an extension of the lines already drawn in the form of directionalities and articulations. These lines, inscribed by the elementals, mark various regions within the interspace of earth and sky; in this connection the line of the horizon is paradigmatic, for it marks by differentiation the greatest regions, earth and sky. The regions delimited by the elementals constitute places in their broadest expanse, or, more precisely, they constitute protoplaces. Among these are the places that Aristotle coordinates with various elements (for example, the upper region, sky or aither, as the place of fire).

Both protoplaces and places proper are delimited spaces. They are delimitations of luminous space and, more immediately, delimitations of the interspace between earth and sky. Places in the proper sense are more closely delimited, breaking up the expanses of the protospatial regions; yet, more decisively, such a place is the place of a thing rather than that of an elemental. More precisely, a place *can* be the place of a thing, a place occupied by a thing, yet it need not be. Though at any particular time—or even indefinitely—a place may be devoid of things, its very sense of place depends on the connection between place and things.

What is this connection? It might be supposed that the place of a thing measures the same as the thing, that is, that the place and the thing are congruent. If a place is the place of some thing, then it would—by this supposition—be completely occupied by the thing. While places are stationary, things can move from one place to another, but both before and after they move, they fill entirely the place where they are. This conception is formulated more rigorously by Aristotle: place is "the boundary [πέρας] of the surrounding body at which it borders on the surrounded one"—that is, place is "the first motionless boundary of what surrounds."[25] Under the assumption that it is air that surrounds a thing (though it could be, for example, water), its place would be defined by the border where the air touches the thing, that is, by the line circumscribing the thing.

And yet, if things are regarded, not according to the abstract schema of a thing as simply the bearer of properties, but rather as they concretely show themselves, then the congruity will be disrupted, and the place of a thing will prove to exceed the thing. For in the self-showing of a thing there is always operative a horizon of other things that, like a halo, surround the thing; yet, they not only surround the thing but, most decisively, contribute to the very way the thing shows itself, that is, they coconstitute its manifest appearance. They form a peripheral horizon that shades off as the removal from the thing increases; but as belonging to the manifestation of the thing, which is inseparable from its very being, this horizon belongs to the place of the thing. Since, in turn, the

---

25. Aristotle, *Physics* 212a4, 21.

periphery shades off indefinitely, there can be no circumscribing line; the place of the thing has no strict border but extends indefinitely beyond the circumference of the thing. It is like a sound that grows softer and softer and that will eventually become silence, yet in such a way that one cannot simply mark the point where the sound finally gives way to silence. It is like the sound of the bells, which grows ever quieter as one takes distance from the cathedral, yet in such a way that there is no determinable point where the sound is no longer heard. It is also like the place of the human body, which in its comportment always exceeds the mere boundary surrounding it. So it is with the place of things, with place as it exceeds the mere boundary of things and enters into the self-showing of things.

Once the place of things is expanded by way of the peripheral horizon, it can no longer be supposed that, while things typically move from one place to another, places remain stationary. For when things move, when they shift even slightly, their peripheral horizon is reconfigured. As a result of this reconfiguration, the place of a thing moves along with the thing, even if its movement does not exactly match that of the thing.

Yet, even if no reference is made to the self-showing of the thing, the supposition that, while things can move from place to place, places remain stationary still proves untenable. Since to say that places are stationary is to say that a place is always in the same place, the statement recoils on itself: it entails that place can have a place where it remains in place. In other words, it entails that place presupposes place, that there is a place anterior to place.

Once the sense of place is referred to self-showing, it becomes evident that the place of a thing moves, not in some hypothetical anterior space but along with the thing, not by passing from one place to another—thus presupposing itself—but rather through the shifting and configuring of the horizon structure.

To an extent the place of a thing merges with the self-showing thing. The primary difference is that the horizontal structure belongs, as a moment, to the place, whereas for a thing it is not a moment, not a component, but rather merely contributes to the self-showing of the thing. While horizontal structures are gathered around the thing and are necessary for its appearance, what shows itself is just the thing itself. Horizons plot the way to the thing but in the end recede and let the thing itself come forth in its own manifestness; they let the thing show precisely itself, let it show itself as itself. The space of this self-showing is the final determination of luminous space, the terminus of the entire series of determinations.

D. Self-Showing

The progression from luminous space to earth, sky, and the other elementals, then to the articulation and differentiation they introduce, then to the lines that constitute place, issues finally in the formation of the space of the self-showing of things and those self-showing things themselves.

How, then, do things show themselves? What are the structures that constitute the space of self-showing?

Things show themselves from out of horizons. The peripheral horizon consists of the immediately surrounding things, some of them well-defined, others merging into an undifferentiated expanse. On the one hand, this horizon is a primary moment in the structuring of the space of self-showing. On the other hand, the horizon is not what is to appear but only a moment that, in part, enables the appearance. As it adheres to the thing so as to frame its appearance, it must also be disengaged so as to let the thing itself come forward into appearance. The simultaneity of coming to adhere to the thing and of disengagement from it defines an almost unheard-of bonding of opposites. One name for such holding together of opposites in their opposition is imagination.

Yet, within the peripheral horizon, the thing itself does not simply, directly appear. What is immediately presented is only a profile of the thing; it is the face, as it were, that it turns to a particular exterior vantage point. Though it is through a profile that at any particular time a thing shows itself, it does not coincide with the profile. Rather, as a profile is presented, there is covert reference to all the other profiles that the thing could present to other vantage points. The totality of these other profiles constitutes the lateral horizon of the thing. Although a thing presents only one profile at a time, the profile may continuously give way to another (especially if the thing is in motion); in this case the horizon, too, shifts as a new profile is presented and the previous one is reabsorbed into the horizon. A thing can, then, show itself only through a profile and from out of the horizon of all other possible profiles. In this case, too, as with peripheral horizons, there is a yoking together of opposites, for the lateral horizon is both apprehended and simultaneously not apprehended, both withdrawn from vision and yet integral to it.[26] Here, again, the proper name of such bonding is imagination.

In addition to the horizons, there are other factors that exercise an effect on the appearance of a thing. Lighting is primary among these factors. The color of a thing varies depending on the intensity and the color of the illumination. It will also show a different look if a shadow is cast across it. There are also material factors that have a certain effect on, among other instances, the color of things. There is perhaps no better expression of the entire range of this kind of effect than that offered by Merleau-Ponty:

> This red patch that I see on the carpet is red only by virtue of a shadow that lies across it; its quality appears only in relation to the play of light upon it. And hence as an element in a spatial configuration. Moreover, the color is definite

---

26. See my extended analysis of horizonality in *Force of Imagination*, 106–17.

only if it spreads across a certain surface, too small an area not being describable in these terms. Finally, this red would literally not be the same if it were not the "wooly red" of a carpet.[27]

Though such phenomenological descriptions are largely oriented to vision and visibility, there are horizon structures operative in events of self-showing geared to other senses and other sense-forms, though for the most part the articulations of these structures are more indefinite than in the case of visible things. A tone may sound different when heard from different vantage points. The sound of an organ played in a small chapel will not be the same as when it is played in a huge Gothic cathedral. The texture of a piece of velvet will appear different depending on the direction in which one runs one's hand across it.

Things are self-showing, things of many kinds, some discrete and well-defined, others merged into an indefinite expanse, some entirely exposed to vision, others holding themselves in part reserved, conserving their secret strength. All show themselves from out of their horizons, which is to say that they appear within the place they occupy.

While their fully concrete appearance is not reducible to mere self-showing, while self-showing belongs within a structure constituted by abodes and customs, self-showing marks the inception of appearance, which is compounded by the further complex. Thus, self-showing must first be brought into focus before examining its expansion into the full event of appearance.

In regard to things as self-showing, there are two connections that are originary. The first of these is ontological. Things never simply *are*. In that they are, they are also self-showing. As soon as a thing is, it can be observed; it can show itself to one capable of apprehending it as the thing it is. There is no sequencing between being and self-showing; it is not as though a thing first comes to be and then, in sequence, gains the capacity to show itself. Self-showing belongs originarily to it in that it *is*; self-showing is concurrent with its very being. Although it belongs essentially to self-showing that it *can* take the form of self-showing to someone, it is not necessary that it take this form. Even in the absence of an observer, the thing will remain self-showing, even if in a privative mode.

And yet, even if the observer can be absent, even if there is no observer, it belongs essentially to the thing that it shows itself to someone. This is the second originary connection, that of self-showing with the possibility that there is one to whom the thing shows itself.

---

27. Maurice Merleau-Ponty, *Phénoménologie de la Perception* (Paris: Gallimard, 1945), 10.

An actual occurrence of a pairing, in which a thing shows itself to one who apprehends it, constitutes an *event of manifestation*. And yet, this pairing is not a mere juxtaposition; the one to whom the thing shows itself is not simply a self-contained recipient apart from the event and the self-showing thing but rather enters projectively into the place occupied by the thing and lets itself be drawn into the spread of horizons while also remaining itself. As drawn to the peripheral horizon, the perceiver is cast toward a panoply of things configured in a coherent pattern and shading off at the extremity. The very constitution of the lateral horizon already installs an intrinsic connection with the one thereby drawn to the thing in its self-showing; for the profiles that make up this horizon are coordinate with the various perspectives taken by the one whose observation is thereby drawn to the thing. The very sense of profile is tied to that of perspective. Merleau-Ponty has analyzed the engagement of the perceiver with the perceived in his investigation of sensation. In order to undermine the traditional theories according to which the observer would be merely a passive recipient of sensation, he appeals to the fact that sensations such as those of color have inherent motor meaning; that is, they provoke incipient movements. The implication is that the very reception of sensations already involves a response by the subject. It is not even that sensations are given and that then there is a response, but rather that the giving and the response are inseparable moments.[28] Thus, there is an intertwining of sensation and reception. As one comes to see a distant object, one, at the same time, focuses one's eyes to accommodate the distance, casts one's vision into the distance; one does not first receive an image of the object and then adjust one's vision accordingly. In broader terms, the observer is always already engaged with the things that show themselves and indeed is already caught up in the event of manifestation.

In its capacity as self-showing, a thing occupies its place; it shows itself from out of its place. Yet, since the observer is engaged with the thing in its very self-showing, since the observer is engaged in that self-showing, the observer, too, is adherent to this place, even though always maintaining a withdrawn reserve. Since place and, in particular, the place of the thing are the result of the series of determinations of luminous space, the thing occupies not just its place but the entire series of openings, which expands from place to elementals, preeminently earth and sky, and then finally to luminous space. This sequence of ever broader openings within which self-showing occurs constitutes a *site of manifestation*. But, in turn, since the observer is engaged with the self-showing of the thing, the observer will also—though not without reserve—belong to this series of openings. This configuration of openings to which both the self-showing thing and the observer, in their intertwinement, belong constitutes the *full site of manifestation*.

---

28. See ibid., 242f.

E. Abidance

Things never simply appear, for to their appearance there belongs a complex structure intrinsic to the event of manifestation and its site. Around things that are to appear, lateral and peripheral horizons are gathered, and it is only from within these horizons that things can appear. Since the spread of the thing to its horizons (inclusive of them) constitutes place, it can as well be said that a thing can appear only in and from out of its place. Extending from the thing, the horizons shade off into various elemental articulations set within the region delimited by earth and sky. Movement is not simply between stationary places (places that remain in the same place) but rather is such that the place of the thing is borne along in the movement; and if change of place (now understood as the movement of place) must have reference to something relatively more stable, this can only be to earth and sky, preeminently to earth. Furthermore, as things appear in and from their place, and thus within the space of earth and sky and, in the broadest reach, within luminous space, the beholder is necessarily engaged with their self-showing, and conversely, such that there is between them an intertwining. Such is, then, the full expanse of the site of manifestation.

And yet, humans do not live solely within events of manifestation; neither do things show themselves solely at the corresponding sites. Such a site could never be one at which a sacrifice to the gods could take place in accord with the customs to which those who participated—or failed to participate—were bound. Neither could such a site be one at which custom, enforced by legal imperative, would require the banishment of a transgressor from a certain place. These are sites or expanses where humans abide and where they are, in varying degrees, bound by customs, which provide them with the orientation and measures that make possible the accordant judgments, decisions, and actions that life requires. *Abode* and *custom* are two of the numerous senses borne by the word ἦθος. The affinity between these senses, encapsulated in the word, can be discerned in these examples: it is always within a particular abode that the constraints—but also the enabling capacity—of custom are operative.

An abode is an expanse in which things present themselves in a guise that exceeds that in which they would show themselves to straightforward apprehension, a guise in which they are transformed from that which they would display on mere sites of manifestation. An object that to a detached observer appears as merely a stone becomes, within a certain abode, an altar on which the inhabitants of that abode offer sacrifices to the gods.

Humans find themselves within certain abodes. They first come to themselves there, yet without any living memory of how they came to be there; they simply find themselves unaccountably there. Even to say that they are thrown there presupposes that there occurred a motion by which, though without a manifest agent, they came or were brought to be there. But one has no sense of having been caught up in a motion by which one would have come there but only of finding oneself there, of having always found oneself there as far back as memory can reach.

Humans recognize, even if only tacitly, that they belong to a community, that their lives unfold within a polity, that they rely upon and are never entirely apart from nature, that they are exposed to the elements and thus require shelter, and that virtually all that concerns humans takes place in the open space between earth and sky. Their very self-awareness is inseparable from their finding themselves there in the nest of abodes.

The figure of a circle, of concentric circles, or, dynamically conceived, that of an expanding circle offers an appropriate mathematical representation. Emerson begins his essay "Circles" with these words: "The eye is the first circle; the horizon which it forms is the second; and throughout nature this primary figure is repeated without end."[29]

Habituation is never lacking. An abode grants orientation to the complex of directives by which one can take one's bearings in relation to oneself, in comportment to others, and in the awakening of wonder at all that—as with the cosmos at large—exceeds the reach of humans. Certain abodes harbor exceptional danger, exposing one to forces beyond one's control, as in the threat of retribution by the gods. From others one may have been compelled to take flight, lamenting then the lost abode that could have provided shelter. Others offer a space in which a more youthful temper can be enjoyed, even if only for a time.

As being-with-oneself, one necessarily belongs to the proximal abode, no matter what degree of self-oblivion or self-evasion may cloud one's awareness and impede transparent reflection. Moreover, as encircled by—nested within— the other abodes, one is stretched toward them, distended across them. More generally, regardless of which abode one is centered on, regardless of one's emplacement, one is stretched out toward the broader abodes and retracted toward the narrower abodes. One's centeredness can be disrupted by such threatening events as the onset of war, the approach of a severe winter storm, or the outbreak of a pandemic; it may give way to emplacement in another abode, so that the entire patterning of abodes is altered.

As one remains within one's proximal abode, one may, at the same time, become attentive to one's being stretched to the extreme and may then fix one's gaze, for instance, on a star, which, though utterly inaccessible, offers its light to the vision of the most solitary wanderer. One lives both with oneself and under the starry heaven above.

In order that one's vision and one's engagement be stretched to the abodes beyond that of one's ownmost self, imagination must be operative; it must extend

---

29. Emerson, "Circles" in *The Selected Writings of Ralph Waldo Emerson*, ed. Brooks Atkinson (New York: Random House, 1940), 279.

or enlarge what is actually present, what is concretely presented, so as to open vision and engagement of whatever sort to the abode as such. One does not actually see a city as such but only buildings, groups of people, streets, and so forth. Likewise, one does not see nature and its elements as such but only landscapes, trees, animals, and the like. Imagination must extend what one sees to encompass the abode as such and thus to render it visible, as we say, to the mind's eye. As regards nature, in particular, it is a matter of renewing the ancient distinction between nature (φύσις) and natural things (τὰ φύσει ὄντα) and of regarding them as linked by the operation of imagination.

And yet, since they necessarily abide in nature, humans are exposed to its destructive forces. It is largely because of this exposure that shelter is imperative, that it is a basic necessity of human life. Shelter can take many forms, ranging from the most direct, as in barricading oneself, to others in which one takes refuge in the memory of an earlier abode that provided comfort and safety and in singing like a nightingale about the irretrievably lost abode. If, like Metis and other legendary figures, one is driven from one's abode, then the memory of that abode may issue, not in surrogate shelter, but in bitterness at being forced—as by blows of fate—into flight and exile and at being compelled to seek a sheltered—and perhaps final—refuge. Giving voice to Apollo's oracle, Oedipus recalls a future once foretold and now become present:

> He told me of all my miseries to come,
> Spoke of this respite, after long years,
> In the final land,
> A resting place among the sacred Furies.
> There, he said, you shall round out your bitter life,
> A blessing to those who receive you,
> A curse on those who have driven you away.[30]

Almost as a point at the center of the nest of nearly concentric circles, there is the abode that one has with oneself. As being-with-oneself, one is both self-identical and divided within oneself, corresponding both to a point and to its expansion into a minuscule circle, the least of those that shape the nest of abodes. Yet, this almost infinitesimal separation from self bodes one's installment, always already, in community. In turn, pluralizing of communities and the resulting conflicts, both within and without, portend the emergence of political life, which, set apart from nature, is nonetheless dependent on its resources. Beyond, there is the circle never yet—perhaps never to be—measured, the circle that puts in question whether there is an outermost limit or whether there is only drift without center or bound.

---

30. Sophocles, *Oedipus at Colonus* l.87–93.

There are manifold ways in which humans abide in these circles. They may also venture onto a path that would lead beyond them; or, more precisely, they may seek transition into an entirely different dimension. Their venture is directed to a hidden veil—a concealed concealment; they will never succeed in simply, without further ado, lifting the veil, since it is itself veiled. The veil is thought to cover that which lies almost beyond the reach of humans and of which there is offered, at most, no more than a brief glimpse. Even if one could catch sight of the gods, their retreat on Olympus lies far above the planes of mortals and, receding behind a veil of clouds, remains utterly withdrawn from human vision.

The circles are resistant to deformation and yet endure it. While retaining their figure as circles, they also harbor an excess that deforms this figure through extension beyond itself. Each abode overreaches itself, laps over onto others, especially those that are contiguous with it. The smooth surface of a lake can reflect clouds in the very midst of nature. Communal bonding may stabilize or disrupt the corresponding polity, which, in turn, may recognize or suppress the communities within it.

Each circle is thus deformed into a spiral, or, in stricter terms, into two spirals almost coincident except that one opens upward to the superior abodes, the other downward to the inferior ones. Yet, while deformed into a spiral, each remains also a circle, since the circular figure is what defines the abode. Thus, each abode retains its identity as a circle while also overreaching itself, differentiating itself from itself, spiraling toward contiguous circles, which also are subject to such deformity. The configuration displayed by each abode is that of two noncongruent figures, a spiral imposed on a circle. Each abode can overreach itself, can spiral toward others, only if it also remains itself, only if it persists as the abode it is.

The configuration is that of a spiral that is also a circle or of a circle that, only by remaining itself, can become—must become—a spiral. Both circle and spiral constitute a single abode. They do not occur separated from one another but as centered in exactly the same space in a seemingly unrepresentable coincidence. It is only by force of imagination, determined as the power of holding opposed terms together in their opposition, that this double figure can be sustained. In this way and to this extent, imagination is operative within each and every abode.

It is as with the Empedoclean roots: each has its proper region and force, yet each can encroach on the others, producing a heterogeneity that, regarded more generally, resembles that generated by the superimposition of one figure on another not congruent with it.

Human abidance is not only a matter of presence, of simply being present in an abode, of passively occupying it. Rather, as the word suggests, to inhabit an abode is also to bode something (or, in the obsolete form, to abode it). It is to portend, to foresee, to be attuned to what is promised in one's abidance—as when one says of something that it bodes well. In other words, to inhabit an abode is also to be engaged by and in possible disclosure within the abode. Within the spiraling circle of an abode, one abides portentously, disclosively. Abidance entails openness to disclosure.

* * *

The polyphony of ἦθος is like the music of Palestrina. Listening attentively to the word, one hears several melodically independent voices, which sounding together, produce a harmonious concert. One voice sings of abodes, some that last forever, some only dreamed of, some offering shelter to wandering strangers. Another sings of custom, of how it binds together those sharing a common abode, of how, in its cruelty, it has driven some from their abode, of how it can expose an entire community to retribution. Still another voice sings of character, of how one's abode shapes one's character, of how one's character is framed by custom, of how, in confrontation with impending death, all disguises may fall away and one's true character may be revealed.

The songs of the Ancients in praise of ἦθος continue to resound. Homer sings of how Telemachus, accompanied by Athena on his search for news of his father, displayed his fine character in the strange abode where they disembarked. Socrates sings of those rare judges capable of penetrating all disguises so as to creep into a man's soul and reveal his true character. Another Athenian, unnamed, sings his Dionysian songs, praising wine for its capacity to disclose a man's character and for its power to reverse the order of time and allow the affective temper of youth to be temporarily restored. And Socrates sings of music itself, recalling that on the previous day he explained to Glaucon how music instills in the youth the highest virtues belonging to excellent character.

3   Solitude and the Stars

A. Palintropic

In the first place there is intimacy. One always has a sense of oneself, of not being apart from oneself, of being close to oneself. To this being-with-oneself there corresponds one's proximal abode. This abode is delimited by one's proximal reflection, by one's turning apprehensively upon oneself. In one direction this abode, this space of the self, represents a remote limitation of luminous space itself. In another direction this abode spirals beyond itself in such a way that it proves to be circumscribed by more extensive abodes; thereby a nest of abodes is configured.

It is the prospect of securing oneself within the proximal abode, of coming to be most closely with oneself, that can entice one to seek solitude. If one could enter into solitude so as to be alone with oneself, one would have achieved a self-reliance bordering on finite absoluteness, and the song to be sung would be a song of oneself.

Emerson is the emissary of being-with-oneself. He writes: "I am always environed by myself."[1] He is also the herald of solitude. In his words: "To go into solitude, a man needs to retire as much from his chamber as from society."[2]

How, then, is intimacy operative? What figure does proximal being-with-oneself assume? The figure that is traced is that by which the self engages reflection, turning back on itself in order to apprehend itself, in order that it be disclosed to itself.

In its reflective turn, the self is spaced apart from itself, only then to be brought back to itself as apprehended in the turn. This self-differentiating that is healed in the return to self constitutes the dynamics of the turning and the dynamism of the self as such. And yet, the turning cannot consist only in this dynamic; for in the space of the reflection, there must occur a disclosure of the self to itself. In the return to self, an apprehension of the self is delivered to the self.

---

1. Ralph Waldo Emerson, "Character," in *Selected Writings*, 370.
2. Emerson, *Nature*, in *Selected Writings*, 5.

The turning of the self upon itself delimits the proximal abode; it traces the outline of the abode. To abide is to circle within the periphery of the circle inscribed by the circling from oneself around to oneself. The abode of self-reflection does not have the form of an inner receptacle or a sphere of subjectivity. Rather, while circumscribing the circuit of self-reflection, it stretches beyond itself both as spiraling out through the nest of abodes and as opening to the elements—the proper elementals—that, reflecting back upon the self, determine human propriety.

There are three traits of the reflective self that are decisive. The first consists in the self's irreducible singularity: one belongs inescapably to oneself. The self upon which one turns in direct self-reflection is exclusively one's own self. Furthermore, it is by reference to oneself as one's own that something can be owned. Such owning provides the basis for property, which, to the extent that it is linked to human singularity, takes the form of private property. Property as such constitutes a bond connecting the circuit of self-reflection, in its ownness, to a dimension beyond the range of self-reflection.

The second trait consists in the differentiation of the self from inanimate things. Whereas a thing simply *is*, a self both *is*—regardless of the operative sense of being—*and is aware* that and, to some degree, how it is. Only a self can turn back on itself so as to disclose itself to itself, whereas no disclosive space opens within things; they remain fully compact.

The third trait concerns the elusiveness of the self. In the turning, the self apprehends itself, not, however, as something substantially present but as withdrawing, as fugitive. In turning to itself, in pursuing itself, the self does not ever quite catch up with itself. There always remains that which, as withdrawing, remains undisclosed in reflection. In that on which reflection is brought to bear, there always remains concealment, and thus reflection can never get in its purview itself as a definite, integral whole.

There may arise the prospect of coming to enjoy one's being-with-oneself with enhanced intensity. Achieving this intensity requires that one withdraw from all that would compromise the abode of self-reflection. By clearing the abode in this manner, it becomes a more rarefied space in which one can intensify the turning on oneself, "living" in it to the exclusion of everything else, concentrating one's attention in such a way as to penetrate beyond the normal limit of disclosure, peering further into oneself. Such intensified reflection constitutes solitude.

Emerson attests to the bounding by which a clearing for solitude can be established. In his first book, *Nature*, he begins with words already introduced above: "To go into solitude, a man needs to retire as much from his chamber as from society." He explains why such retirement is required in order to achieve solitude: "I am not solitary whilst I read and write, though nobody is with me."[3] Such are, then, among the requirements for solitude: one must withdraw not only from society and thereby from the intrusion of alien moments into one's own abode but also from the engagement with language that reading and writing involve. Whatever form it may take, even that of monologue, language lets a shared voice sound within one's abode. In the interest of solitude, the attraction of language must be resisted. Even if words sometimes insinuate themselves into one's abode, they must be kept at a distance—silenced or left unsaid, not even entertained or at least deferred beyond one's time of solitude. During this time one must withdraw from speech, setting oneself apart from it, disregarding and resisting all enticement to speak or to call up what is intended from speech or writing. Thereby one's self-reflection is freed to itself. Solitude can commence only to the degree that one's turning upon oneself is restricted to a proximal abode purged of alien moments, which, borne especially by language, would intrude on it. Within such an abode, one can turn upon oneself with a purity and a force beyond that which is normally operative, extending thereby the range of the self's self-disclosure.

Emerson also describes the opposite affect, the inverse of solitude. It is no less exceptional than solitude. It is broached when, in an extreme ecstatic leap, one transgresses the limits of one's proximal abode and becomes oblivious to this abode. Muting one's self-reflection, one abandons oneself to circles that lie entirely outside the nest of abodes. In "Circles" Emerson writes:

> The one thing which we seek with insatiable desire is to forget ourselves, to be surprised out of our propriety, to lose our sempiternal memory and to do something without knowing how or why; in short to draw a new circle. Nothing great was ever achieved without enthusiasm. The way of life is wonderful; it is by abandonment.[4]

In light of this description, the question that imposes itself concerns the bearing of solitude on the achievement of such ecstasy: Is it perhaps precisely solitude that is capable of casting one most forcefully into the affect of ecstatic abandonment? Is it perhaps the case that one must be intensely with oneself in order then to be transported beyond the circle that is one's own?

Emerson's exposition expresses the fact that solitude is not the only form of exorbitant comportment: at one extreme the self is utterly concentrated, while at the other extreme there is open abandonment and the joy of wonder. Indeed, Emerson does not by any means advocate unconditional and unlimited withdrawal

3. Ibid. The further, related citations are taken also from the initial paragraphs of *Nature*.
4. Emerson, "Circles," in *Selected Writings*, 290.

into solitude. He hints that for all the richness that solitary meditation can afford, it can, if overly prolonged, come to border on vacuity. In a journal entry dated June 12, 1838, only two years after the publication of *Nature*, he writes:

> Solitude is naught & society is naught. Alternate them & the good of each is seen. You can soon learn all that society can teach you for one while. . . . Then retire & hide; & from the valley behold the mountain. Have solitary prayer & praise. Love the garden, the barn, the pasture, & the rock. These digest & correct the past experience, blend it with the new & divine life, & grow with God. After some interval when these delights have been sucked dry, accept again the opportunities of society. The same scenes revisited shall wear a new face, shall yield a higher culture. And so on. Undulation, alternation, is the condition of progress in life.[5]

In his essay on Plato, Emerson emphasizes still more the significance of undulant motion, of alternation, of transition to and fro. He regards this exigency as imperative for poetic creativity. He writes: "Our strength is transitional, alternating." More specifically, he refers to: "the experience of poetic creativeness, which is not found in staying at home, nor yet in travelling, but in transitions from one to the other, which must therefore be adroitly managed to present as much transitional surface as possible."[6]

And yet—solitude is neither ecstatic abandonment nor incessant transition. Rather, as the intensification of being-with-oneself, it requires the exclusion of any alien, intrusive moments that would compromise its proximal abode. Even if it is such that it will eventually, inevitably, be drawn into a transition to the public sphere or even inversion into abandonment, it is, as such and as long as it persists, exclusive of all that, from without, would limit self-reflection. Even if, as Emerson suggests, solitude may in some instances involve a certain attunement to nature, it is from out of one's solitude that this attunement will have been released, and consequently solitude will remain intact as such.

Yet, it is questionable whether the exclusion of all external moments suffices to induce solitude. It would seem that even with the clearing of its space, an enticement is needed in order to intensify being-with-oneself into solitude. Emerson identifies a unique enticement capable of drawing one into solitude. It is an enticement that comes from afar. The very vision by which one is drawn closest

---

5. Joel Porte, ed., *Emerson in His Journals* (Cambridge, MA: Harvard University Press, 1982), 187.
6. Plato's capacity to remain in transition between two moments so as to command both is one of the primary themes in Emerson's interpretation of Plato. Following the passage just cited, he writes: "This command of two elements must explain the power and the charm of Plato. . . . Plato keeps the two vases, one of aether and one of pigment, at his side, and invariably uses both. . . . Plato turns incessantly the obverse and the reverse of the medal of Jove. . . . In him the freest abandonment is united with the precision of a geometer" ("Plato; Or, the Philosopher," in *Selected Writings*, 479–80). This essay is from *Representative Men*, published in 1850.

to oneself is directed at a site utterly remote from one's proximal abode. Emerson writes: "But if a man would be alone, let him look at the stars." He explains how the stars, in their very remoteness, can have the effect of drawing earthbound humans into solitude: "The stars awaken a certain reverence, because, though always present, they are inaccessible."

The implications of Emerson's connecting solitude to the vision of the stars are decisive. A star—any star, all stars—is beyond our reach. Furthermore, it bears no reference whatsoever to any of the things and persons that otherwise would always threaten to intrude upon and disrupt one's solitude. If, in looking at a star, one engages oneself entirely in this vision, all else falls away, including, for the most part, the other stars surrounding it; the same detachment is displayed by each and every star on which one's vision focuses and even from all the stars that are visible, which appear as configurations of points of light set against the blank darkness of the nocturnal sky. If, in relation to the stars, one is entirely engaged in vision, the accounts that have been given of the stars, whether mythological or scientific, have no pertinence at all. Around the star there is no horizon but only darkness, visible negativity. Moreover, there is no possibility of assuming other perspectives such that through projection of the corresponding virtual profiles the star would be objectively presented. One sees a star always from the same perspective, which is to say that perspective plays no role in the vision of the star. In any case, the mere point of light presented to vision of the star can offer no profiles; a point of light is the same regardless of the angle from which it is seen.[7]

Emerson's appeal to the stars has significant consequences. By fixing one's eyes on the star, one is drawn more intensely to oneself, drawn into solitude. It is especially consequential that solitude is attained, not merely by turning upon oneself more discernibly or more exclusively, but rather, above all, by casting one's vision into the distance, away from oneself, beyond to the very limit of vision. By gazing away from oneself, by looking outward to the extreme limit, to what is immeasurably remote, one is driven into the utmost proximity to oneself. Being-with-oneself becomes most intense, becomes solitude, by means of the most exorbitant vision.

It is also significant that the form in which a star appears is unique: it lacks all the qualities that belong to all other things. It displays itself as nothing but a point of light. It is as if it were pure illumination completely apart from all that it would illuminate; it is as if it displayed a site of illumination where everything

---

7. In modern astronomy triangulation is often employed to measure the distance to a star. The base of the triangle is formed by the moving earth, that is, by the line connecting two successive positions of the earth. The sides of the triangle converge at the point representing the position of the star. Yet, even when in this way the perspective changes corresponding to the end-points of the base, the star still appears, not in different profiles, but as a point of light.

extrinsic had been stripped away. As light thus purified, the star is set against a space that, unlike that of the diurnal sky, is enshrouded in darkness and offers almost nothing to vision. In the appearance of the star, there is a regression through the entire sequence of determinations of luminous space, a regression leading back to an intimation of luminous space as such. The star is, paradoxically, like the heavy fog on the coast of Maine. Just as the fog, growing thinner and beginning to dissipate, attests to luminous space, so, as the star fades into the coming day, the dawn's growing light and expanse of colors offer an intimation of luminous space; for "when primal dawn spread[s] on the eastern sky her fingers of rosy light," a sense of luminous space is awakened.

Still another consequence concerns content: in this regard there is a correspondence between the appearance of the star and the constitution of solitude. The star does not exhibit any extrinsic qualities or properties of the sort characteristic of things. Its only features are intrinsic to it: since it appears as a point of light, these features pertain exclusively to its luminosity (for example, the intensity of its light, its periodic or continuous shining). In solitude, likewise, there is a lack of extrinsic connections, a withdrawal from both familiar places and from the social relations that structure the everyday lives of humans and, above all, from language with its compromising commonality. On the basis of this correspondence, the star, indeed the entire nocturnal sky with its myriad of stars, appears as a visible paradigm of solitude. It demonstrates solitude and in the reversion of its light can engender self-disclosure to one who is visually attentive.

Emerson attests to such display of solitude. Again, his words: "But if a man would be alone, let him look at the stars."

It has also been attested—in antiquity—that beyond all other powers possessed by vision, the capacity to behold the starry heaven is the greatest good of vision. Gracious acceptance of the highest gift of vision can take place only in and through responsive beholding of the stars. The ancient declaration that the order displayed by the stellar paradigm can be reflected back upon the turning within oneself remains, in a certain respect, pertinent. And yet, the discovery in recent astrophysics that beyond the range of unaided vision there reigns not only disorder but also forces of destruction and creation so enormous and so strange that even the designation *phenomenon* must be withheld renders problematic—though not necessarily insignificant—any reflection back upon the human.

Whereas the scientific discovery of the previously unsuspected complexity of the cosmos poses a broad range of unprecedented questions, certain forms of human intrusion undermine the paradigmatic role that the stars formerly played in the lives of earthbound humans. In particular, the clarity of Emerson's vision is threatened by the enormous number of satellites—soon to number in the thousands if there is no intervention—that corporations are in the process of launching into low orbits, for from their solar panels they reflect light back to the earth's surface as if they were stars. The consequences of such stellar pollution can be foreseen from the outset. Not only can these fake stars create serious obstacles to astronomical research (for instance, by amplifying the normal ambient light) but also they can interrupt the unaided observation of the stars that is common to humanity, that produces a kind of extended solar community among humans. In particular, the paradigmatic role played by the points of light in the night sky will be largely cancelled; contrary to Emerson's account of the stars, these bright satellites will not be inaccessible nor necessarily always present; neither will they display the more complex features that modern research has revealed. Some astronomers, distressed by this development, have predicted that eventually—perhaps even in the near future—these semblant stars will outnumber the genuine ones, at least those that can be seen by unaided vision. There is assurance that even just a few hundred of these satellites will inhibit observation of constellations, that is, of stellar configurations of which all humanity, both present and past, have shared a common view. The irony could hardly be greater than in a statement by a representative of one of the corporations involved in launching the satellites: he declares that the project is for "the greater good"—oblivious, no doubt, to the fact that he is virtually quoting the expression in the *Timaeus* in which observation of the starry heaven is declared the "greatest good" (μέγιστον ἀγαθόν) of vision.[8] And yet, it is evident that the greater good that would be served by the satellites is not the good of humanity at large but only that of the corporations in their drive for ever-greater profits. Fundamentally, however, the situation stems neither from the technology that produces the satellites nor even from corporate interests; rather, at the deepest level, the situation is governed by politics, by the political, capitalist sustaining of a world in which—as one scientist puts it—"there are multibillionaires with the ability and the desire to do things like this."[9]

Such intrusion is also an infringement of ethicality. Stellar pollution violates something that belongs in common to all humans. Such debauchery robs humankind of the joy, elation, and sense of measure wrought by beholding the starry heaven. In obliterating the free view of the panoply of stars, such virulence violates the stellar or cosmic imperative. It disrupts the very bearing of the upper elemental abode and more broadly that of the cosmic abode that all have in common and that binds all to the universal community.

B. Mutation

Emerson's description of ecstatic abandonment testifies in the extreme to the transition that, while not breaking all bonds with the circuit of self-reflection

---

8. See the account in *New York Times*, June 4, 2019, section D, 1, 3; and Plato, *Timaeus* 47b.
9. This statement, cited in *New York Times* (see note 8), is by the astronomer Tyler Nordgren, one of the principal advocates of the preservation of night skies.

and to abodes, leads beyond it. This transition is effected by a mutation of self-reflection by which, though, on the one side, remaining intact, it is, on the other side, reconstituted outside the circuit. In specific terms, the circuit in which the self turns upon itself mutates into a reflective circuit in which the self turns to an other, to something other than itself—most directly to inanimate things and finally to other humans. As one reaches out to an other, as one touches the other, whether with touch, with vision, or through speech, the other reflects back to the self a certain self-understanding. The reflective circuit conjoining the self with itself mutates into a circuit conjoining self and other. Moreover, the differentiation between the self and itself in the one circuit is carried over to the mutated circuit as differentiation between the self and the other. Because of this differentiation, neither self nor other can be assimilated to the opposite term. There is perhaps no more perfect example of this irreducible difference than that provided by Emerson's description of the way in which a star to which vision is extended can induce solitude.

The circuit of reflection produced by this mutation is not one of objectification. The star as touched by vision is not an object at all but only a point of light. Moreover, the circuit of self and other is not assimilated or appropriated to the circuit of self-reflection To be sure, the star shines and in this way conveys itself back to the viewer; but it does not come to show itself as nothing—or almost nothing—but an objectification of the viewer, a mirror functioning only to reflect the self back to itself. Neither is the star an objectification of human activity such as labor; neither is it something that will eventually have given way to such objectification, contrary to what has in some instances been said in reference to nature. Again the words of Emerson: "The stars awaken a certain reverence, because though always present, they are inaccessible; but all natural objects make a kindred impression, when the mind is open to their influence."[10]

When, within the mutated circuit, one reaches out to an other, the reflection back upon oneself does not empty the other of all distinctive content, of all content native to the other. Rather, the other reflects back to oneself from out of its alterity; that is, it holds itself back, withdraws from all attempts to capture its innermost core and to reduce it to utter negativity or to determinate negation. Whether the other is a thing, a person, or some other animate being, it effectively shields itself from the panoptic vision that would violate it.

Within the circuit of self and other, the other to which one reaches out—in an event of manifestation—reflects back on oneself; it grants a certain self-understanding the form or level of which is determined partly by the way in which one reaches out and partly by the identity of the other. The reflection is

---

10. Emerson, *Nature*, 5.

simplest in the case of things. All things point back to oneself from their place apart from oneself. From their location, mere things (natural or crafted) point to one's own location amidst things. It is as if, with their semblance of vision, they looked back at the viewer, as if they emitted a ray of light that illuminated the place from which they were seen. This double connection between viewer and viewed is governed, for the most part, by the correlation between the perspective of the viewer and the profile that the thing presents to one viewing it from that particular perspective. In showing itself through a particular profile, the thing indicates the perspective from which it is viewed and to that extent reveals the location of the viewer.

Reflections of this kind occur also in the exercise of other modes of sense, though the directionality is normally less precisely indicated than in the case of vision. A sound heard may indicate one's distance from the source of the sound and, though less precisely, the direction from which, in one's location, the sound is heard. The limit cases of reflection are taste and touch, which are sometimes taken to be, in fact, closely related.[11] In touching a velvety fabric, for instance, there is virtually no separation—hence minimal reflection—between the touching and the touched, even though one can never quite touch oneself touching.

Paintings often display concretely various forms of reflection back upon the viewer. Many portraits, for example, are composed in such a way that as one looks into the eyes of the figure portrayed, the figure appears to look back at oneself. On both the side of the viewer and on that of the portrait, there is the double structure of seeing and being seen. Just as the viewer both sees the portrait and appears to be seen by the figure therein, so in turn, the figure both is seen and appears to see the viewer. The formal structure is thus such that the dyad on the side of the portrait is the inverse of that on the side of the viewer. But with regard to content, there need not be such correspondence. The seeing that is seen in the portrait does not necessarily evoke a sense of identity (or of correspondence of another sort) with what is seen in the portrait. In other words, the reflection does not in most cases simply transfer to the viewer what is seen seeing in the portrait. For example, a figure who displays excessive pride and a look of presumed superiority[12] may evoke a sense of opposition to a social order that condones such posturing as a privilege of an upper class. At the other extreme, the look of destitution as the members of a hopelessly impoverished family are gathered around

---

11. Most notably by Aristotle, who, comparing taste with smell, writes that "we have a more precise sense of taste because it is a certain type of touch, and that is the most precise sense a human being has" (*On the Soul* 421a).

12. A paradigm of such a figure is shown in Frans Hals's *Portrait of Jaspar Schade* (c. 1645). See my discussion in *Logic of Imagination*, 131–33.

a table on which there are only the most meager provisions[13] may evoke a mood of sadness and sympathy at the plight of those represented by the figures in the painting, or it may evoke outrage against the social forces that are responsible for reducing human life to such a base level. The spectacle of elemental nature, whether directly observed or seen as it is depicted in a painting, can reflect back to oneself an affective sense both of one's belonging to nature and of the force and expansiveness of human imagination. Gazing upward at overpowering mountain peaks, one may gain a sense of one's own sublimity, as if drawn upward in spirit.[14] Or if, standing on a high rocky ledge, one gazes—like a wanderer—out across a sea of fog, the view may awaken an awareness of the vast reach of human vision and of the boundlessness of imagination.[15]

In his account of his Italian journey, Goethe describes the primary purpose of his travels: "I am making this wonderful journey, not merely to occupy myself, but to come to know myself in the objects I see."[16] The objects of his vision are not just mere things, but primarily the brilliant artworks and the grand edifices that, as he writes, were "built for eternity."[17] The specific reference is to what he saw in Rome; it was there especially that he found something of himself, that something exceptional was evoked by what he saw. He writes: "Now I turn back into myself. As one likes to do on every opportunity, I discover a feeling that gives me unlimited joy and which I venture to express. Whoever looks seriously around him here and has eyes to see must become sound [*solid*]; he must grasp a concept of soundness [*Solidität*] that was never so lively for him."[18] Goethe's voyage is one of

---

13. The reference is to Vincent van Gogh, *The Potato Eaters* (1882). A critic, van Rappard, initially friendly to van Gogh, stated that this work "terrified" him. His criticism led to a hostile exchange and a break in the friendship between van Rappard and van Gogh. See Douglas W. Druick and Peter Kort Zegers, *Van Gogh and Gauguin: The Studio of the South* (Chicago: Art Institute of Chicago, 2011), 37–39. Van Gogh's comments hint at the way in which the picture might appear terrible to one who lacks the keenest vision and thus is unable to see the light within the darkness. In a letter to Theo, written while he was still in Holland, van Gogh says: "one of the most beautiful things done by the painters of this country has been the painting of *black*, which nevertheless has *light* in it." Mark Roskill, ed., *The Letters of Vincent van Gogh* (London: Fontana, 1983), 226. In another letter to Theo, sent from Arles, van Gogh refers to his portrait of Roulin the postman and writes: "The coloring of this peasant portrait is not so black as in the 'Potato Eaters'" (276). Yet granted the blackness of the *Potato Eaters*, van Gogh indicates that there is light in it. His sister-in-law, who championed his art, reports his saying that the painting is "from the heart of peasant life" (64).

14. A prime example is Caspar David Friedrich's *TheWatzmann* (1824–25). See Joseph Leo Koerner, *Caspar David Friedrich and the Subject of Landscape* (London: Reaktion Books, 1990), chap. 10. See also Kant, *Kritik der Urteilskraft*, Bk. II, esp. §30.

15. The reference is to Caspar David Friedrich's *The Wanderer above the Sea of Fog* (c. 1818). See my discussion in *Senses of Landscape* (Evanston: Northwestern University Press, 2015), 65–76.

16. Johann Wolfgang Goethe, *Italienische Reise* (Frankfurt a.m.: Fischer, 2009), 47.

17. Ibid., 143.

18. Ibid., 143–44.

self-discovery. The exquisite works of art that he experienced in Rome cast their brilliance back upon him, arousing a joyful feeling in which he gained insight into himself. The grand edifices, built for eternity, displayed for him a soundness that, reflected into himself, would—almost paradoxically—never have been so lively. It is this lively soundness, this sound vitality, that he discovers and welcomes when he turns back into himself. This turn has nothing whatsoever to do with an unmediated retreat into subjectivity.

In the case of self-portraits, the operative structure is more complex, and the configuration of moments does not constitute merely a direct reflection from nature or from art. While the artist—Rembrandt, for instance—looks at the image of himself in the mirror, that is, the image cast back to his vision from/by the mirror, he does not merely apprehend the image but recasts it as a painting. It is in this recasting that the artist exercises his creativity. There will be a certain identity between the painting and the image, and if the mirror is a smooth, regular surface, the image will have the same look as the artist; otherwise it will be distorted. But what is most decisive is that the creativity of the artist will always install difference within the identity joining image and painting. The painting will never have simply the same look as the image. Thus, even if the mirror accurately reflects the artist, there will necessarily be an unbridgeable difference between the look of the artist and the look displayed by the painting. Strictly speaking, a self-portrait is impossible.

This divergence is expressed by David Pollard in his dense poetic idiom circling around Rembrandt:

Skin and paint are different stuffs
as he was a different species from himself
reflected. What he knew he was
skated along the sliver of light
the mirror bent, refracted, resurrected
into the image of a stranger.
. . . .

These images were born in thoughts of his departing
and in the horror of identity, of selves, of ruins,
of messages from the dead
for what God did with words he did with paint,
breathing his spirit
into himself out of the darkness
like a halo.[19]

---

19. David Pollard, *Three Artists: Parmigianino, Caravaggio, Rembrandt* (Belfast: Lapwing Publications, 2017), 52.

And yet, a self-portrait, like any portrait, offers more than immediately meets the eye. For when the artist brings his creative spirit into play along with his finely tuned skill, the aim is not distortion but truth in the sense of bringing to light certain features that otherwise would have remained hidden; painting does not simply reproduce the visible but makes visible. When most successful, a (self-)portrait can reveal inner dispositions or even the depth of character, indeed in a manner not entirely unlike that which—though in an extremely more rudimentary way—can be brought about by the means represented by Dionysus. In his self-portrait the artist sees himself differently and, in the finest instances, more truly than in the mere mirror image.

Yet, both reflection from things with their horizon of profiles and reflection from the artist's mirror, however complex, pale by comparison with the reflection that comes back to oneself from other persons. It is a reflection that not only offers a moment of self-understanding but also evokes an enactment of that which one is given to understand. Another's look of joy can call forth a sense of one's own, perhaps previously passive, joyousness, which, in turn, may be enacted in a corresponding deed. On the other hand, reflection from another may yield an image that diverges from one's own self-understanding but that, precisely through the divergence, can activate and enhance certain aspects of one's own self-understanding.

Never is another person entirely other. Even in a cross-cultural, multilingual context, a sign of forbearance is likely to bring a response, perhaps welcoming, perhaps hostile, perhaps from behind what one discerns as an invisible mask. Only rarely will one fail to reach another in some manner and to have a reflection conveyed back upon oneself. For another person is never unqualifiedly other, totally alien, utterly foreign, never in the way that death, robbing one of oneself, is other. In the mutual comportment of persons, there is no absolute alterity. Always there are grounds for hope that the threshold of community will be attained.

C. Infinities

The stars, which, to the human viewer, are capable of inducing solitude, are utterly removed from anything human; in Emerson's phrase "they are inaccessible." As indefinitely exceeding the human, they offer perhaps the most immediate exemplification of infinity in the precise sense in which it has been redetermined, indeed in a form that, unlike the dialectical concept, allows the finite to be sustained in its opposition to the infinite. According to this redetermination, the infinite—as concretely manifest—is defined as whatever surpasses the human immeasurably, whatever *exceeds humans indefinitely*, without limit. The infinite is the ἄπειρον as it bears on events of manifestation.[20]

---

20. This redetermination is carried out in *Logic of Imagination*, 201–4. On the dialectical concept of infinity, see Hegel, *Enzyklopädie der philosophischen Wissenschaften*, Dritter Teil: *Die Philosophie des Geistes* (Frankfurt a.M.: Suhkamp, 1970), §28, *Zusatz*.

To observe the stars in the manner described by Emerson is, at the same time, to engage the intense being-with-oneself offered by solitude. This engagement takes place by way of a turn outward rather than through turning merely upon oneself. One's vision leaps over the entire sequence of abodes, according attention neither to the community to which one belongs nor to one's civic domicile, leaving them behind, springing over them as if in freely chosen exile. Looking outward from oneself by looking upward, gazing so far into the distance that even the concept of distance begins to unravel, one disregards even terrestrial nature, even the earth itself. There remains in view only the sky, which, covered by darkness, offers only the slightest indication of the cosmos beyond. All that appears are mere points of light. Otherwise there is only the nonappearance of space as it would be before becoming luminous, that is, in a time not only before time but also before light, before even the possibility of appearance as such. Thus, the leap over the sequence of abodes is also a leap back over the entire series of determinations of luminous space, from the place of the manifestation of things to luminous space and even beyond to space as such. Much the same holds, inversely, of the reversion by which from the pure vision of the stars solitude can be induced; the reversion passes over all that otherwise mediates between these two terminal moments. These inverse transitions exemplify the courses—the double oppositional directions—that are requisite in order to avoid the one-sidedness of proceeding either solely from the human or solely from the cosmos. Both courses must be followed, even though within certain intervals one may remain merely tacit: both the course stretching from space as such to the self-reverting human and that extending from the proximal human abode to cosmic space.[21]

In the configuring of the self's full propriety, a mutation is the decisive factor. As in the first such transition, it is the circuit of self-reflection that undergoes mutation, but whereas previously the result was a circuit of the self and a finite other (a thing, a person), what issues from this second mutation is a circuit of the self and infinities. In other words, it is a circuit of the self and the elementals that pertain to the self. This circuit is, as previously, a circuit of reflection: the self reaches out toward and is drawn by the elementals, and, in turn, the elementals reflect back to the self a certain self-understanding. Again it is Emerson's solitary vision of the stars that offers a paradigm of the circuit; for the stars shine forth precisely as announcing the elemental cosmos, which by way of the stars reflects back to the self that more profound understanding of being-with-itself that is conveyed through the intensification that constitutes solitude.

---

21. This requirement can—despite the enormous and unbridgeable differences—be regarded as a transposition of the demand for inverse transitions between transcendental philosophy and philosophy of nature. The necessity of such transitions was first—and most succinctly—formulated by Schelling. See F. W. J. Schelling, *System des transzendentalen Idealism*, in *Schriften von 1799–1801* (Darmstadt: Wissenschaftliche Buchgesellschaft, 1967), 339–52.

As infinities, as exceeding indefinitely the self itself in its ownness as the proper, the elementals bear on the self. These infinities along with the finite, reflective self constitute the propriety of the self as such. It is only in its full propriety that the self can enter into the circuit of self and other. It is only as already borne on by the elementals that the self can sustain reflective exchange with an other.

The most absolute elemental is death, which dissolves the entire round of being-with-oneself. Death robs one of oneself, forces oneself totally away from oneself. Death is absolute alterity; it is the coincidence of ownmost and othermost, the event in which one's ownmost becomes othermost, in which one becomes absolutely other than oneself; it is, in this sense, the dissolution of oneself. And yet, as ever impending possibility, death is not only the other than oneself but also is the other *of* itself; as other than itself, it concealedly haunts oneself. It exceeds oneself indeterminately and yet bears on oneself. It is infinite, yet in its excess it releases a reversion, casts a reflection, back upon the finite self, a reversion that discloses to oneself one's utter mortality.

The most palintropic, though no less effective, of the elementals is birth. In its relation to the self proper, birth is two-sided. On the one side, it is a gift, indeed the gift of all gifts, the gift that opens a space for all possible gifts. It is in being born that one is given to oneself, that, paradoxically, one is bestowed upon oneself at a moment when one would previously not have been oneself. Birth is not a matter of production, as though the self were fabricated through the sexual act or its medical surrogates. It is not even just a matter of generation, of *Geschlecht* (in every sense): birth installs one within a human nexus, within, for example, an allegedly racial identity, an order of ancestry, and a familial community; it is not so much that one is thrown into this nexus as that one finds oneself unaccountably there. The arrival of the pure gift, as well as all that first issued from it, is entirely beyond remembrance; it is completely inaccessible, irretrievable in every sense. As pure gift, birth retreats from all disclosure, from all mnemonic recovery. These retreats constitute the indeterminate excess of birth, the infinity that harbors the reflection through which humans become aware of their natality.

The most broadly extending elemental is nature, primarily as it is concentrated and expanded in the natural elements, in earth and sky, in mountains and ranges of mountains, in thunder and lightning, in the fierce wind and heavy snow of a winter storm. Humans belong to nature not only as comporting themselves to it but also as harboring nature within themselves, within their bodies. Humans are *of* nature, and their abodes are circumscribed by the natural elementals, preeminently by earth and sky, which delimit the space in which almost all that matters to humans takes place. Hesiod's Golden Race was exemplary in the blessed way they abided within this space, bounded by the sky where Cronos then reigned, and the earth, which provided them with abundant fruit so that they lived like gods without sorrow and toil.

The most abyssal of the elementals is seclusion, which has also been called the unruly and an interminable night. It is an unfathomable depth, and though, like all elementals, it is installed in a circuit of reflection with the self, it eventuates as an interruption of reflection, as a concealing of the self from itself, as a withdrawing of the self from itself, as impeding—and finally halting—the self's passage to itself, as constituting a limit—itself unstable—beyond which reflection cannot penetrate. Seclusion undermines the self-possession that an unbounded reflection—if it were possible—would attain. It is, then, primarily seclusion that renders the self fugitive. Even in solitude, in stretching one's apprehensive powers to their greatest extent, seclusion eventually comes to block further disclosure.

There is no telling what may have disappeared into seclusion, or what may have been held there entirely undisclosed, or how what is held in seclusion may have determined, have intruded on, what comes to light in the self's reflection on itself. On the other hand, without the veil being lifted, there may well up into self-reflection vague images, obscure connections, errant thoughts, even creative initiatives that otherwise would have remained sheltered within the negativity of this profound retreat.[22] What seclusion reflects back to the reflective self is the abyssal limit of reflection and hence the limit of self-disclosure.

In the context of his speculative psychology, Hegel describes such a concealed depth, such seclusion, as a nocturnal pit in which infinitely many images are preserved without actually being in consciousness. He specifies that one does "not have full command over the images slumbering in the pit of my interiority [*im Schacht meiner Innerlichkeit*]." He adds: "No one knows what an infinite throng of images of the past slumbers in him."[23] Despite the evident affinity, the present discourse is, in several respects, quite distant from Hegel's as regards this concealed depth, which is accordingly designated primarily as *seclusion*. Over against Hegel's account of the nocturnal pit as inward, as belonging to interiority, it is, in its abyssal depth, regarded as exceeding the self. Moreover, that which is contained in the pit—if the concept of containment is possible here—is limited neither to images nor to things from the past.

Each of the elementals is inscribed within a reflective circuit that derives from a mutation of the circuit of the self reflecting on itself. Thus, each elemental belongs within a circuit in which the other moment is the reflective self. The finite

22. The affinity between seclusion and the Freudian unconscious has been analyzed in *Logic of Imagination*, 222–28. Central to this analysis is the demonstration that Freud cannot—or at least does not—avoid granting to consciousness a certain privilege, that ultimately he conceives the unconscious processes primarily as duplicating the structure of the conscious processes. This demonstration provides the basis for rigorously differentiating seclusion from the unconscious.

23. Hegel, *Enzyklopädie der philosophischen Wissenschaften*, Dritter Teil: *Die Philosophie des Geistes* §453, *Zusatz*.

self is exceeded indefinitely by the four infinities, the proper elementals, that bear upon it.

This bearing involves two reciprocal moments. One moment consists in the bearing of the self toward the elemental: this moment is not, as might be supposed, a projection upon the elemental; for, with only one apparent exception (nature), an elemental is not itself present such that one could project upon it. Rather, the self is drawn toward, attracted to, the elemental, and then in a certain proximity imagination is brought into play so as to make visible to a kind of vision the otherwise invisible elemental.

The other moment lies in the reflection of the elemental back upon the self in such a way as to grant to the self a certain self-understanding. For one who is receptive to this gift, the self-understanding takes place as recognition and formation of oneself, as reorientation, as a turning around, as παιδεία.

Reflection from death as elemental offers a recognition of one's mortality. It can issue in a reorientation in which one becomes overtly aware that death belongs to life as its limit, that all who are born must die their own death. Such reflection is sedimented in the Greek mythical contrast of mortal humans with immortal gods. In similar fashion the attraction toward birth is paired with the granting of a reflection on oneself as determined by natality. The space between these two elementals, along with their respective reflections, constitutes the course of life, which is a peculiar mixing of mortality and natality and which, as it unfolds, also grants self-understanding. The ancient testimony to the wisdom of old age is not entirely amiss.

The prodigious profusion of the presence of nature exercises the most intense attraction. The beauty of nature, the boundless grandeur of the natural elements, the fecundity of the earth—these cannot but reflect back to humans the understanding (whether recognized or not) that they belong to nature, that they are *of* nature, and that nature is not only outside but also within the human.

Seclusion displays a direct opposition to nature in that it is precisely the limiting of presence, that it is a withholding from the light. Yet, one who is receptive cannot but experience wonder at the upsurge from the darkness. Thus, drawn to it and giving it its peculiar visibility through imagination, one may reflect on the hidden depth of the human, on what has been called—by St. John of the Cross—the dark night of the soul.

D. Corporeity

In its being-with-itself, the self can become visibly manifest to others and even to itself only *as a body*. The positing of this identity, semantically qualified by the *as*, cannot but broach—has always broached—an interrogation aimed at revealing the moment of difference by which the identity is qualified.

Despite the fact that character has to do primarily with the self, it sustains also a connection with the body. Since the self becomes manifest in the appearance of the body, certain moments of a person's character will also appear corporeally, and consequently the exposure of a person's character does not necessarily require that one delve beneath the person's exterior appearance. Character is not, then, a quality entirely hidden away out of sight.

While one's body is sensed as one's own, its ownness is derivative from that of the self. Schelling writes that the body "only becomes *my* body through the capacities to think and to will"[24]—that is, through reflective activities belonging to the self. While remaining my body, the body can require supplements in cases of injury or disease, indeed supplements that neither simply are my own nor are not my own. A vital organ can be transplanted in one's body; the organ is then one's own and yet not one's own.

At the symposium scripted by Xenophon, there are several persons—Charmides, Critobolus, and Niceratus—whose love affairs are described by Socrates; their underlying characters are thus expressed, put into words. But there is one—Hermogenes—whose character is not merely expressed in Socrates's discourse but rather is described as actually apparent, as visibly manifest in certain discernible features. In effect, Socrates issues to those present an invitation to observe the features in and through which Hermogenes's character appears: "Do you not see how serious his brow is, how calm his gaze, how modest his speech, how gentle his voice, how cheerful his demeanor?"

In regarding Hermogenes's calm gaze, in looking into his eyes, Socrates would have seen him seeing, would have perceived the look in his eyes. He would have observed this union of seen and seeing, not as merely an object seen but as an event of animated receptivity.

That which animates one's gaze and at the same time appears therein has been named—in a complex history of translation and of evolving linguistic forms[25]—ψυχή, *anima*, *âme*, *Seele*, *soul*. The most succinct formulation comes from Hegel: "But if we ask in which particular organ the whole soul appears as soul, we will at once name the eye, for in the eye the soul is concentrated, and the soul does not merely see through it but is also seen in it."[26]

Yet Hermogenes is also characterized by the seriousness of his brow and the cheerfulness of his demeanor. The word translated here as *demeanor*—namely,

---

24. F. W. J. Schelling, *Ideen zu einer Philosophie der Natur*, in *Schriften von 1794–1798* (Darmstadt: Wissenschaftliche Buchgesellschaaft, 1967), 375.

25. The Modern English *soul* goes back to the Middle English form *soule*, which, in turn, developed from the Old English form, *sāwo*, which is akin to the Old High German form, *sēule*, from which evolved the Modern German form, *Seele*.

26. Hegel, *Ästhetik*, ed. Friedrich Bassenge (West Berlin: Das europäische Buch, 1983), 1:155–56.

ἦθος—expresses perhaps most explicitly the communication between inner character and its outer manifestation. The revealing of Hermogenes's character reaches its highest pitch when Socrates attributes to him a modesty of speech and a gentleness of his voice. It is when speech comes to amplify bodily appearance that character is most openly disclosed. In one's corporeity, demeanor, disposition, and character are outwardly manifest; indeed they are not just passively exhibited but openly enacted.

In all these features Hermogenes's body and not merely his soul is involved; more precisely, each of these features displays in a unique way the identity that conjoins body and soul in their seemingly unfathomable difference. Yet, whereas the human body has, with only rare exceptions, always been thought as animated, there are significations sedimented in the word/concept *soul* that fail to recognize fully the identity, the interpenetration that is displayed in those features of Hermogenes to which Socrates calls attention. While, therefore, the word *soul* has been effaced in the present discourse, the senses that are to enliven this discourse are dispersed into other words and expressions as they function in their appropriate context.

In the *Cratylus* it is none other than Hermogenes who, in the course of the etymologies, asks Socrates about the body, that is, about the name *body*, or, more precisely, about what is meant by the word *body* (σῶμα). Socrates observes that with only the slightest changes the name yields—by way of graphic affinity—three senses. First of all, some say it is the *tomb* of the soul (σῆμα ... τῇ ψυχῆς), as though the soul were buried. Secondly, body is taken to mean *sign* (σῆμα), "since it is by means of it that the soul signifies [σημαίνω] what it signifies." Thirdly, the Orphics believe that the body is like a prison in which souls undergo punishment, that it is an *enclosure* where the soul is *kept safe* (σῶμα).[27] In this instance not a single letter must be altered; this presumably is the reason Socrates says—not without his usual irony regarding Orphism—that it seems to him most likely that they are the ones who established the true meaning of *body*.

In reference to these three meanings of *body*, the most evident difference is that between, on the one hand, the designation of the body as tomb and as prison and, on the other hand, its designation as sign or signifier. To say that the body is the tomb or prison of the soul is to describe it as closed off and hence as confining the soul within itself. But insofar as the soul can convey signs by means of the

27. Plato, *Cratylus* 400b–c. The word σῆμα, which is equated with *body* (σῶμα) and which means sign or signifier, is also used derivatively to designate a sign that marks a grave and thus also comes to mean tomb. Moreover, σῶμα can also be taken as a noun cognate with the verb σώζω, to keep safe, and thus can be taken to designate a place, an enclosure, in which the soul is kept safe or a prison in which it is safely locked up. See *Socrates and the Sophists*, translation and introduction by Joe Sachs (Newburyport, MA: Focus/Pullins, 2011), 178n32.

body, it can escape its confinement by employing the very means by which otherwise it would be confined. If the body is the signifier of the soul, if it provides the very means by which the soul comports itself to what lies beyond its corporeal enclosure, then it is precisely the body that frees the soul from imprisonment in the body.[28] It is preeminently the voice that allows the soul to transgress its corporeity. Thus it is that humans can—in the manner of Hermogenes—reveal their character by means of modest speech with a gentle voice. Conversely, as Socrates tells Phaedrus, one's character provides fertile soil in which the seeds of spermatic discourse can be planted.

Because the owness of the body is subordinate to the owness of the self, unlimited absorption in the body is virtually impossible. One's owness cannot be assimilated to the body, for the very attempt to break with the owness of the self would cancel that of the body. One cannot give oneself over wholly to the body; one cannot sustain the pretense that one is merely one's body. The difference cannot be submerged into identity, as is attested by certain conditions; in illness one distinguishes between oneself and the ailing body, holding oneself in some degree apart from the accompanying impairment or pain. Even in the face of impending death, even as one submits to its imminent occurrence, one never quite yields entirely; it is not simply that death happens but that one dies one's own death.

Whether one can, even for a very limited time, lift oneself above one's body, whether and how by an ecstasis even beyond the wonderful abandonment addressed by Emerson one could set oneself apart from one's corporeity, is most likely undecidable in a theoretical discourse. Still less decidable, indeed absolutely undecidable in such discourse, despite all the narratives that have been invented, is the question of the survival of the soul apart from the body.

Corporeity is constituted through a bonding of seclusion and the proper within a compound of elements, preeminently of earth, to which belong visible manifestness and thereby the capacity to convey signs. Because in corporeity the proper is to a degree set back into a depth of seclusion, one's body is haunted by concealment. Many bodily enactments never enter the light of reflection.

Sexuality is rooted in corporeity and yet exceeds the merely bodily. It is released through the passage from secluded sentience into the open bearing of the reflective self. Specifically, as sexual affection emerges into the circuit of self and

---

28. Ewegen has called attention to the peculiar reflexivity involved in the identification of the body as signifier. He writes: "The body, on this interpretation, is understood as a sign—that is, as a *word* that signifies something beyond itself, namely, whatever the soul signifies or intends. Thus, in looking for what 'body' signifies, they have found that it signifies the very function of significance, that it signifies signifying." S. Montgomery Ewegen, *Plato's Cratylus: The Comedy of Language* (Bloomington: Indiana University Press, 2014), 130.

other, an erotic arc, a luminous halo takes shape. It is like an atmosphere saturated with sexual significance, which merges with the appearance of the other and which at the same time is reflected back upon oneself as a furthering of desire.[29]

The body does not simply occupy space. To be sure, bodily spaces are distinct from space as such, from space as essentially one, and as Kant made explicit, spaces derive from limitation. Already in the emergence of the natural elementals and primarily of the bounds posed by earth and sky, there is the limitation by which interspace is constituted. But the spaces of the things with which humans for the most part deal involve, in turn, limitation of interspace; it is in traversing these spaces that humans carry on their dealings with things. Though these spaces derive from limitation of the interspaces of the elementals, this limitation does not produce rigid, completely determinate borders; rather, each space extends indefinitely beyond the thing that occupies it, shading off as it recedes from the thing. It is likewise with the space of the body. Not only is this space not rigidly circumscribed, but precisely because it is the space of bodily movement, it accommodates the body's motility and thus extends more indeterminately and more flexibly. As the space of the body, it admits various polarizations—as when, in running, one's entire body polarizes its space in the direction of one's feet and legs and openly extends it along one's course. There are also bodily spaces across which different parts of the body are coordinated and communicate—as with the space between the eyes and the hand of a painter.

Music resounds in space, in the interior space, for example, of a great cathedral. Its reception is suspended between self and body. Listeners extend themselves out into the surrounding space, their audition occupying the space. It is not only that listening requires both reception of sound and attention to the configured sequence of sounds received; in a deeper, more comprehensive way, music both induces ecstasy, drawing one out of oneself, and, at the same time, reverberates throughout one's body. The occurrence of such reverberation may also be regarded as a moment in the performance of dance, as indicated by the names that are common to music and dance.

Things may show themselves in such a way that certain possibilities are envisioned, and these, in turn, may elicit deliberation, decision, and action. The self that is operative in action must be bodily present (even if indirectly) to those things on which certain effects would be produced. Likewise, the self that envisages possibilities in relation to things must be bodily present (even if remotely) to those things. The conation in which one actively engages things or possibilities is to be contrasted with desire. The directionality of desire is nearly the opposite of

---

29. The basis for a productive exchange with the psychoanalytic theory of sexuality is provided by the discussion of the relation between seclusion and the unconscious in *Logic of Imagination*, 216–30.

conation: instead of an engagement of the self with things and possibilities, desire transitions from things and possibilities to the self. It is a response, a submission, to what attracts: things required for mere sustenance, sexual attraction, the beauty of nature and of persons, up to the beauty of art, where desire mutates into ecstasy and contemplation. As long as desire persists, so will embodiment. Only in the states into which it mutates is there a decisive distancing from the body.

What is closest to oneself is the voice.[30] Though vocal sounds are produced by the coordination of certain bodily vehicles—hence a language may be referred to as a tongue—what is uttered by the voice are not—as goes without saying— merely sounds. Aristotle's formulation could not be more succinct: "Voice is a sound that means something."[31] In voicing a sound so as to mean something, one hears one's own voice. Yet, it is from within that one hears oneself speaking; the sound of one's voice as one hears it is different from this sound as heard from without by others, as is attested by the strangeness that one's voice seems to have when one hears a recording of it. In some cases one can hardly recognize the recorded voice as one's own, and often one feels discomfort in hearing this almost alien voice.

The voice belongs neither to one's self-reflection nor to one's own body; it is neither simply one's own nor merely something corporeal. Yet, when one speaks and hears oneself speaking, this circuit reproduces from a distance—from its suspension between self and body—the reflection of the self upon itself. Just as in reflection the self apprehends itself apprehending, so in speaking one hears oneself speaking; and just as the self as turning back upon itself is both identical with and different from itself, so the one who speaks is both identical with and different from the one who hears oneself speaking. The production of vocal sounds is the same as and also other than the reception of these sounds; the person who speaks is the same person as the one who hears the speech, and yet, as speaker and hearer, there is difference between them. This difference can never be simply voided; just as one can never quite touch oneself touching, so one can never simply hear speaking a self that is solely, absolutely, oneself.

---

30. One trait of many animals that constitutes their affinity to humans is that they have a voice, which, on the other hand, contrasts in certain ways with the human voice and varies depending on the species. One thinks immediately of sounds made—though not exclusively—by domestic animals: a dog not only can bark in significantly different ways but also in many cases where the dog is constantly with humans, tends to make sounds that resemble, within the limits of its vocal organs, the speech of humans. In addition, these and other animals often respond, with sounds or gestures, to the human voice, recognizing that something is being addressed to them and discerning in it a sense relevant to them.

31. σημαντικὸς γὰρ δή τις ψόφος ἐστὶν ἡ φωνή (*On the Soul* 420b). Thus, the voice—that is, what is uttered by the voice, by the soul through its voice—is a signifying sound. See my discussion in *Elemental Discourses* (Bloomington: Indiana University Press, 2018), chap. 1.

On the one side, a pure aural presence to oneself (as speaking) is interrupted by the exteriority of the sign that speaking produces, for a sign is a sound that is sounded beyond or outside the circuit of hearing oneself speaking. But on the other side, the self may be intrinsically such that it escapes its alleged containment in interiority and extends itself into the very exterior to which the sign would be banished. In this connection a debate—in their own idiom—could be staged between Derrida and Husserl. If consciousness is pure interiority (as it can be taken to be in the case of silent monologue), then it will be violated by any exteriority such as that of the sign, which has the effect of drawing the voice outward, rendering it external to the self-presence of consciousness. But if, on the contrary, consciousness is regarded as an opening onto exteriority, that is, as intentionality in its most fundamental sense, then, since consciousness would not be a sealed-off interiority, it would not be simply violated by the exteriority of the sign.

E. Character

In its reflection on itself, the self never appears as a self-identical *I* that would persist as the invariant subject of all appearances of things. Still less does it appear as a mere bundle of indivisible perceptions. The self does not show itself either as a substantial subject nor as a dispersed manifold of sense.

Reflection, the self's turning on itself, constitutes the dynamism of the self. This dynamic turning is not, however, identical with the self; rather, the self is what is brought to light in and through the turning. As one turns to oneself, what one discovers is one's self itself. And yet, in the reflection the self does not appear as wholly and determinately present; rather, it appears as withdrawing from appearance, as fleeing from light into darkness. It is a fugitive consorting with—taking shelter within—seclusion. It is not even determinately concealed so that one could measure out a determinate, if partial, appearance with definite bounds and a fixed look.

The formation of character takes place as a stabilization of the fugitive self. The stability is established by positing the self as determinate, as centered within firm limits. Because character emerges through a positing that in some way or other compensates for the suppression of withdrawal, for the stilling of the self's retreat, character can be formed in multiple ways. In other words, there are many forms of character. Emerson describes character accordingly: "Character is centrality, the impossibility of being displaced or overset." A person of character "shall stand stoutly in his place."[32] Character broaches self-reliance, the possibility of a reflection on oneself that does not dissolve into abyssal withdrawal.

---

32. Emerson, "Character," 371. The word goes back to the Greek χαρακτήρ. Derived from the verb χαράσσω (cut, engrave, inscribe), χαρακτήρ denotes an impression cut into something and,

Character is not simply generic; not only are there various forms of character, there is also individual character, which alone is capable of self-reliance. For the formation of individual character, what is instrumental is the self-understanding that is reflected back to the self from the elementals, from the singularity assumed in an individual case by the elementals: my birth is not merely birth in general but *my* birth. It is through this reflection that the individual propriety of the self is formed, and the character of the individual is constituted through a gathering of the singular moments of self-understanding.

Yet, the stability of character is not without limits. While character impedes dissolution, the abyssally withdrawing self endures, as it were, below the surface. While never entirely displacing character, it can resurface and inject instability into one's character, borrowing its force from elemental seclusion, threatening one's character with the prospect of dissipation.

*   *   *

"When they heard this, all agreed not to make the present party a drinking affair, but for each to drink as he pleased.

"'Since, then, it has been resolved,' Eryximachus said, 'that each is to drink only as much as he wants, and there is no compulsion about it, I next propose to dismiss the flute girl who just came in and to let her flute to herself, or, if she wants, to the women within, while we engage with one another today through speeches [διὰ λόγων].'"

"After Socrates had thus spoken, they praised it; and Aristophanes tried to say something, because Socrates in speaking had mentioned him and referred to his speech. But suddenly there was a knocking at the courtyard door that made a lot of noise like that of revelers, and they heard the sound of the flute girl. Then Agathon said, 'Boys, go look. And if it is any one of our close friends, invite him in; but if not, say that we are not drinking but have already stopped.'

"Not much later they heard the voice of Alcibiades in the courtyard, very drunk and shouting loudly, asking where Agathon was and commanding them to lead him to Agathon. Then the flute girl who, together with some other of his

---

more metaphorically, a mark or token impressed on a person or thing, hence, a distinctive mark. The cognate occurs in Middle English (spelled: caracter) as early as the fourteenth century; its meaning at that time was the same as the Greek: impression, stamp, distinctive mark. By the mid-seventeenth century it also designated an aggregate of distinctive features and, more specifically, the sum of the moral and mental features that distinguish an individual or race. By the mid-eighteenth century the word could designate not only a collection of moral or mental features but also the person who embodied the collection of features, and, more derivatively, a personality invested with distinctive qualities by a writer, a personality such as that of an actor on stage.

attendants, supported him and led him before them; and he stood at the door, thickly crowned with ivy and violets, with many fillets on his head. And he said, 'Men, hail! Will you welcome a man who is terribly drunk as a fellow drinker?'"

"And everything was full of commotion, and everybody was compelled—but no longer in any order—to drink a great deal of wine."

"Then Socrates, having put them to bed, got up and went away, and he [Aristodemus] followed, just as he was accustomed to; and Socrates went to the Lyceum, washed up, and spent the rest of his day just as he did at any other time. And once he had passed the time in this way, toward evening he took his rest at home."[33]

* * *

Here a disruptive return, such as can occur when the abyssal self surfaces, is displayed on a larger, multi-character stage. At the outset of the banquet, order (κόσμος) is established, and it is declared with everyone's agreement that order is to be maintained by limiting the drinking and sending away the flute girl, whose instrument, the αὐλός, was associated with Dionysus, madness, and the drinking of wine (usually in excess).[34]

Following the series of speeches delivered almost in the order agreed upon at the beginning, the disruption arrives in the person of the drunken Alcibiades, crowned, like Dionysus, with an ivy wreath. He is accompanied by the flute girl, who was previously sent away. Utter chaos breaks out as a mob of others

---

33. Plato, *Symposium* 176e, 212c–e, 223b, 223d.

34. In Book 8 of the *Republic*, Socrates describes the behavior of a corrupted young man in a democratic πόλις as the practice of "drinking wine and listening to the αὐλός" (561c). In Book 3, he prescribes that those who make or play the αὐλός are not to be admitted to the πόλις that he and Glaucon are building in λόγος, since the αὐλός is the most many-toned instrument of all and hence is not limited to those modes that inculcate the virtues required for this πόλις. Referring in positive terms to the lyre, which was associated with Apollo, he speaks of "choosing Apollo and Apollo's instruments ahead of Marsyas and his instruments" (399d–e). The reference is to the mythic story in which it is told how the αὐλός-playing satyr Marsyas challenged lyre-playing Apollo to a musical contest. Marsyas lost, and he was severely punished by Apollo. Aeschylus attests that the sound of the αὐλός excites madness and associates it with the Maenads, the mad women who followed Dionysus. See Walter F. Otto, *Dionysus: Myth and Cult*, trans. Robert Palmer (Dallas: Spring Publications, 1981), 94.

The αὐλός was not actually a flute. It was a double-pipe reed instrument with three to five finger holes plus a thumb hole in each pipe. The player held both reeds in the mouth and held the pipes apart in a V shape, the left hand fingering one pipe, the right hand, the other. See Don Michael Randel, ed., *The Harvard Dictionary of Music*, 4th ed. (Cambridge, MA: Harvard University Press, 2003), s.v. "aulos" (63). The αὐλός had a shrill, piercing tone and was often played in connection with the singing of dithyrambs in the worship of Dionysus. See Donald Jay Grout, *A History of Western Music* (New York: Norton, 1960), 5.

intrude; order is totally—almost totally—disrupted; heavy drinking commences and continues into the night. And yet, amidst the chaos, order and sobriety do not entirely disappear. They endure in the person of Socrates—as, with the eruption of the abyssal self, character can endure, and its stability can persist. And yet, this endurance and stability, this sobriety, as exemplified in Socrates, did not consist in abstinence, as in the cases of Eryximachus and Phaedrus, who, as soon as the commotion began, simply went away. Rather, in the final scene when only Agathon, Aristophanes, and Socrates are still awake (and the first two are about to fall asleep), "they were drinking from a large cup, passing it from left to right."[35] What distinguishes Socrates is his unique capacity to assimilate the Dionysian eruption; and this is why, as Alcibiades says, "no human being has ever seen Socrates drunk."

Character is a gathering of moments. It most commonly denotes, as in Emerson's description, excellent character; taken in this sense, character is a gathering of noble traits, or, in classical terms, a gathering of virtues. On the other hand, bad character is an assemblage of ignoble or vicious traits. In a derivative sense, the word can designate the person as such who displays noble traits, who has a certain character, or who, as in the theatre, assumes a certain character. Both senses are expressed in the passage in which Aristotle praises Homer: Whereas many poets put themselves forth in their poems, "Homer, on the other hand, after a brief introduction, immediately brings on a man or a woman or some other character never without character, but all having character."[36]

A person's character may be inward, may be kept hidden from sight either voluntarily or habitually, or unknowingly. Plato lets each of two Athenians describe a particular way in which inner character can be exposed. The two ways extend in precisely opposite directions, from outer to inner and conversely. In one direction, there is the case of an able judge who, with his keen perceptiveness, sees into the otherwise veiled interior. In the other direction, there are occasions when wine may be employed to bring out into the open a person's inner character. On the other hand, a person's character may simply be outwardly manifest in corporeal signs such as gestures, posture, facial expressions.

There is a complex connection of character with deeds (as well as, correspondingly, with deliberation and decision). On the one side, carrying out certain kinds of deeds can contribute to the formation or solidifying of a corresponding character or of certain traits or virtues gathered in one's character: "We become just by doing things that are just."[37] Yet, performing just deeds, unless purely by accident, requires that one's character be incipiently just or, at the very least,

---

35. On Socrates's sobriety, see *Rep.* 223c and 220a, respectively.
36. Aristotle, *Poetics* 1460a5–11. All three words translated as *character* are forms of ἦθος.
37. Aristotle, *Nicomachean Ethics* 1103b1–2.

that one be attentive to what constitutes justice. There is also reflection between character and deeds. On the one side, one's deeds reflect back upon oneself, upon one's character; that is, in carrying out certain deeds, one is reflected back to oneself *as* being of a certain character. On the other side, one's character can directly determine the deeds one performs; because one is just, one does things that are just.

As a stabilization of the self proper, of the self's reflection on itself, character is set within the proximal abode. Thus, there is connection between what is designated, respectively, by these two primary senses of ἦθος. Yet, it is not only to the proximal abode that character sustains relations. The character displayed (in many variations) by individuals belonging to a particular commonwealth as it is displayed in their customs (another sense of ἦθος) is linked to their native land, their πόλις, their political abode. The dominant traits of mountain dwellers show connections with the elemental landscape that is their abode. The relation between character and nature is quite consequential, since nature provides means that are necessary for the other abodes in which character is formed and is formative. The relation of character to nature is also compounded by the double—or even plural—sense of the word *nature*. Both the consequential and the compound connections are expressed in two succinct statements by Aristotle and Emerson, respectively. The first: "None of the virtues of character arise in us by nature [φύσει]."[38] The second: "Character is nature in the highest form."[39] The transition between the poles indicated by these two statements would, in the πόλις that is best of all, be brought about by means of gymnastic, music, and the mathematical disciplines—at least in the πόλις that Socrates and Glaucon build in λόγος.

There are also other forms that stabilize the fugitive reflective self, even if not to the same degree as character or its slightly variant mode in the form of temperament. Two distinct forms, akin to, yet different from, character can readily be identified. The first is *disposition*, or, in an outwardly more manifest guise, bearing or demeanor. The second form is *mood*, which, in order to stress its outward orientation, can also be designated as attunement. The three forms are distinguished primarily by their respective temporalities. Once character has been formed, it endures indefinitely, though in the course of one's life it may gradually display some change. Homer's portrayal of Odysseus's loyal son is exemplary; by his persistence in searching for his father, Telemachus demonstrates that he is a man of character, as Athena herself attests. On the other hand, dispositions are confined to limited intervals and thus are more subject to change. The Athenian's

---

38. Ibid., 1103a19–20.
39. Emerson, "Character," 374.

description of how wine can temporarily restore older men to their youth, healing for a short time the austerity of old age, illustrates how one disposition can change into another, even if only for a brief interval; but also it is an open question whether subsequently these men revert to their previous disposition or whether their brief renewal of youth brings out thereafter a new disposition. The third form, mood, is typically of much shorter duration; also moods are more outwardly oriented, more attuned to one's situation and surroundings. The song of the nightingale, her lament for the green leaves left behind, can be designated most appropriately as expressing a mood.

When one says "I am my body" and "my body is myself," the sense of being is destabilized. It no longer signifies either coincidence or identity of two things that are present and present to each other. Since the self continually withdraws itself from itself, since it perpetually withdraws from presence, it escapes the body insofar as the body is simply present, even though, on the other hand, the self can openly appear only as the body. And yet, presence is exceeded on both sides and not only on that of the reflective, retreating self. For the body is no merely passive receiver but rather reaches out to, engages itself with, that which otherwise would be a mere given, passively impressed on the body. Thus, presence is exceeded in two opposite directions: the self retreats from it, and the body reaches out beyond it. At the very simplest, still abstract level, that of mere sensations, there is already corporeal movement, as in focusing double vision on a single object. There is a responsiveness the recognition of which undermines the very concept of a pure sensation and, more generally, the supposition that the body is simply, passively present. Merleau-Ponty has thoroughly investigated this complex and in one of several passages states the result succinctly: "Sensations, 'sensible qualities' are then far from being reducible to a certain indescribable state or *quale*; they present themselves with a motor physiognomy, and are enveloped in a living significance. It has long been known that sensations have a 'motor accompaniment,' that stimuli set in motion 'incipient movements' which are associated with the sensation of the quality and create a halo around it, and that the 'perceptual side' and the 'motor side' of behavior are in communication with each other."[40] Thus, even at the level of mere sensations, the body is no mere passive receiver but reaches out to what sense offers and in this way exceeds the boundary that would otherwise be taken to enclose it. It is not simply a present being set within definitive limits, but rather, it continually surpasses any such limit in its incipient movements toward perceptual objects. Therefore, both the withdrawing self and the outreaching body exceed presence—one vertically, the other horizontally—and thereby escape being posited as simply present to each other. In both cases,

---

40. Maurice Merleau-Ponty, *Phénoménologie de la perception*, 242–43.

the sense of being as delimitable presence is undermined along with the supposition that an identity based on presence exists between them. In this connection it is necessary to dispense with the concepts of identity and difference in favor of those of excessive perceptual engagement and abyssal self-withdrawing.

The exposition of the body that has just been broached prompts a decisive palintropic turn to the protracted discourse, *Force of Imagination*, which began with sense and acknowledged from the outset that a beginning would not simply be achieved. In the manner in which it was nonetheless ventured, the discourse began with sense in its double sense. This ambivalence was delimited by reference to the image as such, which was taken "to signify that in and as which sense comes to be present to sense."[41]

At the present juncture in the continuing discourse, what needs to be recalled is the identification of the image not only as the occurrence and means of sensation but also as the "locus in which the sensible becomes present to sensible intuition."[42] This identification was taken, quite appropriately, as the beginning that was—and yet, as was granted, was not—being launched. But now, turning back to that (non-)beginning and bringing to bear on it the present exposition of the body, it is necessary to recognize that the discourse on the image was only the *beginning from a certain point on* and that at that point it remains imperative to regress to an antecedent beginning, to a beginning before that beginning— hence, to carry out a palintropic turn. For the senses to which the image appears are the senses *of* the body, and thus it is necessary to regress to the *embodied* self, which, as the antecedent locus of the occurrence of sense, is charged with taking up the image so as to comport itself to things.

---

41. *Force of Imagination*, 78.
42. Ibid.

4 Ethicality

A. Measure

Let us return once again to the scene of the cove. Others have now arrived, and they, too, are entranced as they peer into the fog. Gradually, as the fog lifts, they catch sight of the island on the other side and begin to descry the open waters beyond. It is as if their vision, rather than simply being cast across the cove, were taken over by the attraction of the sight and conveyed across the way with almost no effort on their part. They are drawn out of themselves, each individually, hardly aware of one another and yet all there together in the small clearing. Each is for a time a solitary self, and yet, absorbed in one and the same sight, they form a tiny community. They are poised at the threshold of the transition from the self proper to a communal abode.

Drawn beyond themselves, their vision is transported; as the fog lifts and they catch a glimpse of the island across the cove, they are ecstatic. Yet, they have hardly stirred from the spot where they have been standing all along; it is from this spot in the small clearing on this side of the cove that they gaze out into the distance. Ecstasy presupposes stability: one can be transported beyond oneself, losing oneself in what lies in the distance, only if one remains, at the same time, at the place from which the passage beyond is determined. There must be a stable site from which, in ecstasy, one extends oneself; most commonly, this site is provided by one's proximal abode.

Ecstasy is not a rare event that occurs only on exceptional occasions. It is not an event at all but rather a being-beyond-oneself in which one will always already have been installed; it takes the form primarily of an abiding attunement to what lies there beyond. Nothing is more beyond the human than death, which robs one of oneself; it is what is most other, what is othermost. It is not that one pictures the spectacle of death to oneself, not that one summons up an image of one's own death; the would-be representation immediately dissolves itself. Rather, one is drawn to this faceless prospect in such a way that an attunement is sustained. Yet, attunement alone does not suffice to bring about an attentiveness to death. One must surpass the mere intimation into which one is drawn by the tractive power of the invisible look of death. Imagination must come to the aid of attunement, focusing it on the collision of ownmost and othermost, rendering determinate what it could otherwise only intimate. This engagement of imagination is almost as if secluded, and "we are seldom ever conscious"[1] of it unless it is intensified and thereby brought to light.

One is also drawn beyond oneself toward the other proper elementals, toward birth in its remote anteriority, toward the encompassing elements in nature, toward the darkness of seclusion. These elementals belong together in a configuration, which, along perpendicular axes, sets birth over against death and the natural elementals in their bright presence over against the impenetrable obscurity of seclusion. Arrayed in this configuration, these elements, each in a reciprocal exchange with the reflective self, constitute the propriety of the self. In this regard the self is *what it is* only by its relation to elements that it *is not*. It possesses its propriety only by virtue of its ecstatic bearing to elements improper to it. Its eidetic is sundered by the inclusion of the noneidetic array.

While sustaining its ecstasis toward the proper elementals, the self perpetually abides in its indigenous habitation. And yet, the spiraling out across the nest of abodes advances the self also beyond its proximal abode to such an extent that it finds itself to be, at once, an almost solitary self and an inhabitant of the entire space beyond. In being most proximally with itself, it is also, as it were, a citizen of the world.

Thus, along with the ecstasis-inducing elements, there is the dynamic configuration of abodes. Although they are incongruent and hardly intersect, together they release a space that, on the one side, exceeds the human indefinitely and, on the other side, provides humans with sites of habitation, of wonder, of refuge. These two configurations, taken together in their bearing on the reflective self, constitute *ethicality.*

Humans are, as such, submitted to ethicality. In and through the space it releases, it displays the measure of all the measures by which human comportment and discourse are measured. Ethicality constitutes the overarching measure to which every particular measure and system of measures are bound to conform.

The anterior measure provided by ethicality cannot be directly applied to the reflective self in a way capable of eliciting conformity. For the reflective self is intrinsically resistant to order and measure. It withdraws from total, determinate appearance and escapes from all confinement within fixed, determining limits. As fugitive, it inevitably slips away from any measure brought to bear on it, retreating into seclusion.

The self can become fully receptive of measure only if its flight is halted, only if it is stabilized by the formation of character. The transformation of the restive self into determinate character takes place through the reflection of self-understanding back upon the self. The milieu in which the appropriation of this

---

1. ". . . der wir uns aber selten nur einmal bewusst sind. . . ." (Kant, *Kritik der reinen Vernunft*, A78/B103).

self-understanding is initiated consists primarily in custom, as, for instance, in the education of children and in the promotion of certain deeds. Fully developed character requires an individualized distancing of oneself from this milieu. In this connection there is a bond between custom and character, two translations of ἦθος.

By its stabilization the self becomes receptive of measure. And yet, stabilization does not dissolve the unruly motility belonging to the reflective self; it does not eliminate the fugitive but only banishes it, only drives it underground, where it takes refuge under the cover of seclusion. Even as character takes shape within the space released by ethicality and is spread, at least ideally, across the entire surface of the earth, there persists the unruly remainder lurking beneath the surface. If its threat is recognized, the forces of order will struggle to hold it in abeyance, to mount a defense by tightening the bonds of order through rigorous abstinence. Yet, no matter how strong the defense may be, the unruly remainder can break through and disrupt the order and measure established through the formation of character. Drunkenness can dispel sobriety, and unbridled passion can banish reasoned discourse. One name for the unruly as it breaks forth from the darkness of its seclusion is Dionysus.

But short of such disruptive intrusion, measure can be sustained in its bearing on the stabilized self. For the self to be submitted to measure entails its being what it is, in contrast to one whose character diverges from what the person is given to understand as himself. In other words, for the self to be submitted to measure means that its character is determined by its self-understanding. A self thus submitted to measure is an ethical subject.

And yet, the propensity to posit an all-binding system of measure is almost invariably operative, in some instances serving to broaden otherwise excessively restricted and restricting moral codes, in other instances provoking conflict and an irrepressible struggle for dominance leading all too often to violence performed in the name of the good and the just. In contrast to the so-called religious wars all too common in the West, there are strands in the tradition stemming from Confucius (Kongzi) that broach an ethical figure capable of drawing other figures beyond their overly restrictive limits. One such figure is expressed in the word *jen* (仁) , roughly translatable as *benevolence*. *The Analects* reports that Fan Ch'ih asked about benevolence: "The Master said, 'While at home hold yourself in a respectful attitude; when serving in an official capacity be reverent; when dealing with others give of your best. These are qualities that cannot be put aside, even if you go and live among the barbarians.'"[2]

What is unconditionally imperative is that across the entire range of characters there be conformity with ethicality. Such conformity is achievable on the basis

---

2. Confucius, *The Analects*, trans. D. C. Lau (Hong Kong: The Chinese University Press, 1976), XIII/19.

of the reciprocal exchange between the self (stabilized as character) and the moments that belong to the configurations constitutive of ethicality. In one direction there is the attunement evoked by the attraction of the ethical moments; and there is the completion of this movement toward each moment, which is carried out by imagination as surpassing the mere intimation belonging to attunement and as instituting determinateness in the apprehension of the ethical moments. But then in the opposite direction there is the bestowal of a certain self-understanding effected by these moments, namely by the proper elementals and the abodes.

From death as an elemental toward which the self is drawn, a reversion back upon the self is produced, has indeed always already been held in readiness. Through this reversion the self is given to understand itself as mortal, even if ordinarily, and for all ethical moments, little notice is taken of this self-exposure; the self is disclosed to itself in its mortality, in its being bound to die and to reckon in its life with the constant impending of death as the possibility that will rob it of all possibilities and even of itself. From birth as elemental the self is brought to understand itself in its natality; it is offered attentiveness to its finding itself in the midst of life, as always already engaged in the net of society, language, and beliefs into which it will have been born.[3] From the natural elements, which border on full visibility, the self is revealed to itself as encompassed by gigantic, often sublime forces, as cradled but also threatened by these forces, which demonstrate to the self its belongingness to nature. Seclusion grants to the self an awareness that it is divided from itself, concealed to such an incalculable degree from itself, subject to the emergence of what cannot have been anticipated, bound to appear in the seclusive form of a body.

The structure of the reversion is not exactly the same in the case of the nest of abodes, since one inhabits them, directly in the case of the proximal abode but

---

3. This result, that in the self's conformity to ethicality it is disclosed to itself in its natality, provides a decisive means by which to counter Nietzsche's thesis that the basis for subjecting oneself to morality is not itself moral. In *Dawn* he writes: "One becomes moral—but not because one is moral!—Subjection to morality can be slavish or vain or self-interested or resigned or thoughtlessly enthusiastic or an act of despair, like subjection to a prince: in itself it is nothing moral." In the same vein, he declares: "There are no absolute morals" (*Morgenröthe*, in vol. V/1 of *Werke*, §§ 97, 139). Nietzsche's contention is, then, that morality provides no ground—that there is no moral ground—on the basis of which humans subject themselves to morality. To be sure, *if* it were the case that one *subjects oneself* to morality, then Nietzsche's contention would be tautological: before subjecting oneself to morality, one could not have a moral basis for thus subjecting oneself to morality; prior to being subjected to morality, one could have no *moral* basis for anything. *And yet*, no one simply subjects oneself to morality; there is never an act by which such subjection would be initiated. No one performs an act by which to become moral, but rather one is always already subjected to some morality or other. Being moral is not a matter of decision but of natality, for one is necessarily born into a moral code of some kind. It is prescribed by one's natality that one will always find oneself already within a network of morals, regardless of whether and how one might eventually distance oneself from one's natal morality.

also, less directly, as one advances along the spiral path to the other abodes. From within the proper abode, the self is given to understand itself precisely as itself alone, this understanding reaching its pinnacle in the retreat to solitude. From the other abodes the reversion matches in the opposite direction the advance of the self across the entire nest of abodes; the self is revealed to itself as by nature communal, as bound to live in polities (even when resisting such alleged confinement), as belonging to nature and the elemental in nature, and (with a scientific supplement) as adrift within an inconceivably vast and thoroughly decentered cosmos.

It is through the appropriation of these forms of self-understanding that the self comes into conformity with ethicality. Yet, self-understanding is conveyed not only by the moments of ethicality but also in singular reflections, as, for instance, in engagement with other persons. In love one's understanding of who one is comes to be enhanced in a way that it could not otherwise.

From each of the moments of the two configurations that constitute ethicality, there issues a reversion to the self that grants it a certain self-understanding. Yet, the accord with ethicality, the self-understanding that it conveys, is never simply generic. Submission to ethicality in general yields only the measure of all measures; it is the measure that governs—that gives measure for—the singular self-understanding that, reverting from ethicality, provides the basis for all deliberation, decision, and action. It is in conforming to this singular self-understanding, in comporting oneself as one is given to understand oneself, in being, in one's decisiveness, that which one is disclosed as being, in being what one is—that one is an ethical subject in the full sense. For such a subject (which is not a subject but a self that is subjected, placed under—*subjectus*), virtue consists precisely in comporting oneself in accord with one's singular self-understanding. For instance, one's understanding of oneself as mortal is given regressively, not from death in general, but from one's own death, from one's imaginal attunement to one's own death. Again: embodiment is a paradigm in this regard: there is no such thing as the body in general; if construed rigorously, the *the* must vanish, for there is only one's own body.

B. Community

Today most forms of community are threatened. Communities are deteriorating on a global scale, and even those most firmly instituted, such as the family, are exposed to disruptions that put in question their traditional forms. The very sense of community has eroded in the wake of radical theoretical inversions and worldwide political upheavals. It is as if the living spirit that previously informed the concept of community and animated communities at large were in flight. Now one hears that a future community can be foreseen only in the paradoxical form of community without community. The laments over the loss of community and the hopes for newly found or founded communities, while they are laudable, appear misdirected even when they elegantly attest to an exigency to discover a new sense of community.

Never, it seems, has the need to rethink the figure of community been more acute.

The question of community is not one that philosophy has failed to address in a rigorous fashion. The abundant resources thus offered can provide indispensable guidance in the venture to rethink community; they can, in particular, facilitate theoretical openings toward a refiguring of community as abode.

In his deduction of rights, Fichte declares not only that humans have rights only in community but also, more fundamentally, that "the human can be thought only in community with others."[4] Marx links the realization of human talents to community: "Only in community with others has each individual the means of cultivating his gifts in all directions; only in the community, therefore, is personal freedom possible."[5] In specifying that such cultivation will be "in all directions," Marx is contrasting this opportunity with the situation in which the worker is chained to the single, monotonous task assigned him as a result of the division of labor. He draws a contrast also with "illusory communities," which take on an independent existence over against individuals and thereby bring about another form of enslavement.

While, to be sure, it is in solitude that one is most closely, most intimately, with oneself, and while one can indeed be truly with others only on the condition that one is resolutely with oneself, it is in the full actualization of being with others, that is, in community, that one's ownmost personal gifts can flourish.

The minimal condition of community is that a displacement beyond the proximal abode take place, even while necessarily the self remains also in this abode. It is with the appearance of an other that a protocommunity is broached. As an other arrives on the scene (always already), there comes into play a reflection from the other person, which, within the compass of the bond joining the two, offers the self a certain self-orientation and self-understanding. Reciprocity is elicited, and there commences a proper exchange carried out in word or deed. On each side a mutation of proximal self-reflection is carried through: the circuit in which the self turns upon itself mutates into a reflective circuit in which, instead, the self turns to an other, so that the circuit conjoining the self with itself becomes a circuit conjoining the self and the other. While remaining in its proximal abode, the self advances toward a communal abode.

---

4. J. G. Fichte, *Grundlage des Naturrechts*, in vol. 3 of *Werke* (Berlin: Walter de Gruyter, 1971), 112. Originally published in 1796.
5. Karl Marx and Friedrich Engels, *The German Ideology* (New York: International Publishers, 1939), 74.

Beyond the reflective pairing of selves, the most elementary form of community takes shape, namely, the family. Ideally, it is through love that, as Hegel declares, the family is determined. Hegel's description of the moments of love and of its course displays it as progressing from the two united by love to a familial community. He proclaims love to be "the most tremendous contradiction," for in loving another, "I win myself within another person; I count for something in the other, while the other, in turn, attains the same in me"[6]; in other words, love is the most perfect form in which one submits oneself to the other precisely as one is given back to oneself with enhanced dignity and sense of self. In love each reflects back to the other a unique self-understanding in the most concrete and indeed singular sense. It is this "tremendous contradiction" that renders the union of lovers ethical: "The ethical aspect of marriage consists . . . in their love, trust, and common sharing of their entire worldly being as human individuals."[7] In a family into which children are born, in this simplest of communities, love becomes visible: "In the children the union attains an existence in and of itself [*eine für sich seiende Existenz*]."[8] Feeling becomes outwardly manifest.

And yet, the familial community, the home, serves not only to bestow substantiality on the love of the parents but also, of equal import, to shelter the child within a secure abode, thereby providing protection from the open horizons beyond the home and offering security as the child grows into the maturity needed to cope with this broader range of affairs. In addition, the home is the site of early education in the broadest sense, the place where the preparation can commence that is requisite for entering successfully into society. Yet, the ideal has its limits: many children are of course denied a stable familial abode in which sufficient care and opportunity would be available. Moreover, on the positive side, there have emerged today various innovative projects aimed at developing alternative forms capable of providing much that formerly was supplied within the familial home; these alternative sites necessarily house abodes that are not entirely congruent with the domestic abode.

The elementary community constituted by the family sustains only limited duration; as children grow into adulthood, they typically leave the family either to form their own families or to form alliances outside the original family; and though an extended family may perdure for a time, the original, elementary family is fractured and eventually dissolved.

6. Hegel, *The Philosophy of Right*, trans. Alan White and including passages from Hegel's lectures on "The Philosophy of Right," from 1817 to 1825 (Newburyport, MA: R. Pullins, 2002), §158. Among the various German editions: *Grundlinien der Philosophie des Rechts* (Hamburg: Felix Meiner, 1955). Originally published in 1821.
7. Ibid., §163.
8. Ibid., §173.

And yet, there is one community that will never vary as such, despite the continual coming and going of its members; it is an abode that is of unlimited extent and that, with absolute necessity, encompasses all humans, all mortals. It is the community of death. Death is not, as such, communal. In the words of Pascal: "one will die alone."[9] Yet, this is to say that each and every one will die alone, that all will die alone, that *we*, all of us, as the mortals we are, have *in common* the bond to death. As mortal beings we constitute a minimal community, even if most of those belonging to the community have almost nothing else in common with their fellow humans, indeed, even though many will in other respects sustain antagonisms that will set them apart beyond all hope of any further community. And yet, we—all humans—constitute a community of mortals. All belong absolutely to this universal mortal community.

But does the bond to death belong in some manner to the very constitution of community as such? Is human community intrinsically mortal community? Is every community permeated—and ultimately determined—by the power of death, as in the case of the family in which it is the death of the parents that brings about the final dissolution. Or are there other elements that contribute to shaping humans into communities, breaking or at least moderating the hold of death?

It is indeed possible to imagine communities in which death plays little or no constitutive role, communal abodes that are not mortal communities. Still further, there can be—and in fact have been—imagined communities the utopian structure of which would be precisely such that mortality is of little account.

In Shakespeare's *The Tempest*, one of the speeches describes the ideal form of community. The speech is delivered by Gonzalo, the "honest old councillor" to the king. Though Gonzalo's description is not the only presentation of a form of community found in the play, it is the only presentation made explicit in a speech. All the other forms of community that the play sets out, such as that gathered around Prospero at the end of the play, are enacted, are presented in deeds rather than in words.

In his speech Gonzalo describes what he terms a commonwealth, effacing the difference between a community and a polity, or rather, determining the polity precisely as a community, as a perfect community, indeed as the ideal community. He begins his speech in such a way as to signal that all he goes on to describe are prohibitions that would obtain in the commonwealth:

> I' th' commonwealth I would by contraries
> Execute all things, for no kind of traffic
> Would I admit; no name of magistrate;
> Letters should not be known; riches, poverty
> And use of service, none; contract, succession,

---

9. Blaise Pascal, *Pensées* (Paris: Hachette, n.d.), §211.

Bourn, bound of land, tilth, vineyard—none;
No use of metal, corn, or wine or oil;
No occupation, all men idle, all;
And women, too, but innocent and pure;
No sovereignty—[10]

In this speech Gonzalo identifies the commonwealth as a community. This community he describes as one in which all would have all in common. The many would form a perfect unity, a whole in which none would contend with another, thus a whole undisturbed by difference, a perfectly homogeneous whole. All the institutions, practices, or instruments that could set one citizen against another, that would be a condition capable of engendering such contention, or that would be a result of such differences would be excluded. There would be no commerce (traffic) conducive to setting seller against buyer. There are to be no magistrates, since there would be no conflicting claims to be settled. Division would be prohibited between learned and ignorant, between rich and poor, between landed lords and indentured servants, between sovereign and subjects.

The most significant exclusion is that of occupations, which in other commonwealths would provide for the basic needs of life by the use of metal instruments and the cultivation of agricultural products. Thus, there would be no need for labor. All, both men and women, would remain idle.

Yet, even in such a perfect community the basic needs of life would necessarily remain and would have to be provided by some means. Hence, the total exclusion of labor would be possible only if these needs were satisfied in some other way, from some other source.

After a brief interruption by two antagonistic courtesans (Sebastian and Antonio)—dividing the whole speech into two unequal parts, so that its content is enacted—Gonzalo continues by identifying the source from which the basic needs would be satisfied:

All things in common nature should produce
Without sweat or endeavor; treason, felony,
Sword, pike, knife, gun, or need of any engine
Would I not have; but nature should bring forth
Of its own kind all foison, all abundance,
To feed my innocent people.[11]

The basic needs, perhaps all needs, would be satisfied by nature, which would produce everything required to satisfy these needs. Nature would bring

---

10. William Shakespeare, *The Tempest*, ed. Virginia Mason Vaughan and Arden T. Vaughan (Walton-on-Thames, Surrey, UK: Thomas Nelson and Sons, 1999), II.1.148–57.

11. Ibid., II.1.160–65.

forth its products in such abundance that there would be no need for anything to be fabricated by human labor. Thus, all the acts and instruments by which some would rob others of such products would be excluded from this entirely communal commonwealth. In addition, nature would produce all things *in common*. The ideal community would be one in which by nature all would have all in common.

And yet, consequently, such a community would be possible only on the basis of the abundant productivity of nature. In other words, a community of this kind presupposes that nature brings forth in abundance things of its own kind, that is, natural things in distinction from things fabricated through human labor. Should nature prove not to produce such things in sufficient abundance, then such an ideal community could never come about. Labor would prove necessary—as humans cannot survive without food, shelter, and clothing—and, with it, all those institutions, practices, and instruments excluded from the ideal community would be reintroduced. Boundaries would be established to divide the land into a collection of farms, on which labor would be required and over which landlords would keep watch. Metal instruments such as plows to till the soil would become indispensable, and those consigned to farm labor would seldom be free of sweat and endeavor. Once the land is divided, it will become necessary for the boundaries to be protected from incursions; for protection, swords, pikes, knives, and guns will be needed, as well as magistrates appointed to settle the disputed claims that will arise. Gonzalo's commonwealth will unravel completely.

In writing about the good place (εὐ-τόπος) that is no place (οὐ-τόπος), Thomas More does not conceal the affinity of this place, as described by the fictitious narrator Raphael Hythloday (ὕθλος—idle talk, nonsense), with the best of all cities (πόλεις) that, in the *Republic*, Socrates, Glaucon, and Adeimantus build in λόγος. On the title page, just below the expanded title, "On the Best Form of a Commonwealth and on the New Island of Utopia," along with the identification of the author, Thomas More, there is *"A Six-line Stanza on the Island of Utopia by the Poet Laureate Anemolius* [ἀνεμιαῖος—windy, full of wind, from ἄνεμος—wind] *The Son of Hythloday's Sister."* It reads:

> Called once "No-place" because I stood apart.
> Now I compete with Plato's state, perhaps
> Surpass it; what he only wrote about
> I have alone in fact become: the best
> In people, wealth, in laws by far the best.
> "Good-place" by rights I should be called.[12]

---

12. Thomas More, *Utopia*, trans. Clarence H. Miller (New Haven: Yale University Press, 2001), 1.

Even before the actual description of Utopia begins, the affinity with Plato is marked, though contentiously, by the contrast between the possession of private property and the exclusion thereof prescribed by the principle that "all things are held in common," which is exemplified by both "everything Plato imagines in his *Republic* [and] what the Utopians do in theirs."[13] In the narrative, Hythloday, declaring that he spent five years in Utopia, reports that he told the Utopians about "the literature and learning of the Greeks" and that, as they eagerly sought instruction in Greek, he gave them many works by Plato, Aristotle, and Theophrastus.[14]

On the Utopians' island there is no private property; each person is free to pass through the doors into the house of anyone, and every ten years they exchange houses. Gonzalo's account implies the same practice: if, as he says, there is to be no bourn or bound of land, then the land will not be divided into privately owned plots; if there are to be no occupations, if all are to remain idle, then there will be no means, no money, with which to acquire private property. There will be no use for money, and so, like the Utopians, no use would be made of money.

In having Hythloday voice the requirement that private property be banned, More is referring quite directly, if covertly, to the *Republic*. For in a passage in Book 3 in which Socrates is speaking of the guardians, he issues—in interrogative mode—an imperative that is strikingly similar to More's. Here, as throughout the *Republic*, Socrates speaks as the narrator, reporting the events of the previous day: "'Well, then,' I said, 'see if this is the way they must live and be housed if they are going to be such men [the best possible guardians]. First, no one will possess any private property except for what is entirely necessary. Second, no one will have any house or storeroom into which everyone who wishes cannot come.'"[15]

There are a number of corollaries that follow from the prohibition against private property and privacy as such and that are put forth both by Gonzalo and by Hythloday/More. The very first practice that Gonzalo excludes from his commonwealth is traffic, that is, business, commerce. If all have all things in common, then no one would own anything that could be sold to someone else who did not possess it; as a result there could be neither gain nor loss and hence no division between the rich and the poor. Any exchange that might take place will be completely free. Though the Utopians do indeed have marketplaces and warehouses, they are not for the sake of commerce; from the warehouses "each head of household goes to get whatever he and his household need, and he takes

---

13. Ibid., 44.
14. Ibid., 92–93.
15. Plato, *Republic* 416d.

away whatever he wants, paying no money and giving absolutely nothing in exchange"—since "everything belongs to everyone."[16] If all exchange is completely free, then it follows that there will occur none of the otherwise typical disputes, and hence there will be no need for the various means by which normally they are settled. And yet, were private property to be reintroduced, all the differences that Gonzalo would exclude in order that they not disturb the tranquility of his commonwealth would reemerge and would undermine all that he proposes to execute by contraries.

Although the Utopians also ban private property and indeed privacy as such, a repeal of this ban would produce much less severe consequences; for what they also ban or advocate in the wake of the prohibition against privacy is much more moderate than the exclusions that Gonzalo would execute. They do not ban labor or declare it unnecessary but recognize that it is required in order to provide basic human necessities; they ban only the excess of those elsewhere who are constantly in search of luxury. Neither do they ban division of labor, though it is likely that they would resist the redistribution of labor that would be produced by the reintroduction of private property. What is most significant is that, in contrast to Gonzalo, they do not ban knowledge of letters. On the contrary, the Utopians not only allow scholars but give them "total leisure to pursue various branches of learning"[17]; still further, it is from the ranks of the scholars that they choose their rulers. This sovereign, this philosopher-ruler, cares for the Utopians' community, not primarily—if at all—by brandishing prohibitions, but by keeping watch over their communality and, one might suppose, by weaving together in the proper measure the various strands within the community in such a way as to "bring together their life into a common one by unanimity and friendship," so as "to complete the best and most magnificent of all webs, to the extent that this can hold of a common web."[18]

On the other hand, in the project of Gonzalo's commonwealth, there is blatant ambiguity as regards the question of sovereignty—or rather, there is an outright contradiction. In the brief interruption that divides Gonzalo's into two unequal parts, the two treacherous courtesans, Sebastian and Antonio, call attention sarcastically to the contradiction between the beginning of Gonzalo's

---

16. More, *Utopia*, 67–68, 130.

17. Ibid., 64.

18. Plato, *Statesman* 311b–c. There are also magistrates in Utopia, but it is not their task to settle disputes, so that they would be entirely superfluous in a community such as Gonzalo's in which no differences could arise. They do not force anyone against his will but only affirm the benevolence of the community: "since the structure of the commonwealth is primarily designated to relieve all the citizens from as much bodily labor as possible, so that they can devote their time to the freedom and cultivation of the mind. For that, they think, constitutes a happy life" (More, *Utopia*, 66).

speech and the final words he utters before being interrupted. At this point Gonzalo declares that in his commonwealth there would be "no sovereignty." Yet, as Sebastian points out "he would be king on't." Antonio adds: "The latter end of his commonwealth"—that there would be no sovereignty—"forgets the beginning"—Gonzalo's declaration at the outset that "I' th' commonwealth I would by contraries execute all things."[19] To execute all things, presumably with such force as to ensure their enduring stability, is precisely to exercise the utmost sovereignty. Gonzalo's exclusion of sovereignty is itself an act of sovereignty.

There is also a strong contrast between the ways in which the respective communities construe and enact their relation to nature. In Gonzalo's commonwealth there are no occupations; all are to be idle, and the basic necessities of life are to be provided by nature. On the other hand, while the Utopians take delight in being "in accord with nature"[20] and consider such accord to be virtue as such,[21] they do not rely on nature to provide their basic necessities. Though they do not work constantly, they are not simply idle.[22] All are skilled at farming (whereas Gonzalo explicitly prohibits tilth), and thus they supply their food. In addition, each person has his own trade, some working with wool and linen, while all make their own clothing. There are also stonemasons and carpenters. Thus, by the moderate practice of the various crafts, the Utopians provide themselves with the basic necessities of life: food, clothing, and shelter.

The governing principle of such communities lies in the prescription that there be commonality throughout, that all have all in common. This principle requires that there be no property that is not held in common, that there be neither private property nor indeed any privacy at all, which would allow something to be held in store rather than in common. All the practices and prohibitions that cohere to give such communities their character, their distinctive ἦθος, must be in accord with this principle. For every such community much the same description holds as that which Hythloday/More offer of the island of the Utopians: "Thus the whole island is like one household."[23]

Since a household can be regarded as the elementary form of community, this comparison implies that all the fifty-four cities on the island belong to a single overarching community. Whereas Gonzalo effaces the distinction between polity and community by describing his commonwealth as a community, this

---

19. Shakespeare, *The Tempest*, II.1.157–58, 148–49.
20. More, *Utopia*, 84.
21. Ibid., 82.
22. If regarded in relation to the account in the *Republic*, the Utopians' practice in their work could be taken to indicate that they deliberately remain in a "healthy city" of artisans (the first of those built in λόγος) and forgo the transition to the "feverish city" determined by the pursuit of luxury. See *Republic*, esp. 372e.
23. More, *Utopia*, 73.

most comprehensive statement regarding the communal-political structure in Utopia reverses the distinction: rather than communities belonging to a polity, the polity of the island composed of all the cities taken together belongs to a single community. Both the effacement of the distinction and its reversal are indicative of the inseparability of polity and community, of their mutual envelopment.

The character of the community of mortals is thoroughly opposite that of Gonzalo's commonwealth and indeed that of any community governed by the principle that all have all in common; for it is a community in which, as such, none need have anything in common except their mortality. Death individualizes absolutely; it withdraws one from every community, even from the community of being. It withdraws absolutely, absolves one from all bonds that one would have had to others. Death suspends one in absolute nonbeing, from which there can be no reach toward the other. To belong to the community of mortals, to be bound to die, is to be oriented in one's very being—whether knowingly or not—to one's utter withdrawal from community. The community of those who have in common their mortality (and in some cases almost nothing further) is a community constituted by the intimation of withdrawal from community, which is, at the same time, a withdrawal of community from the deceased. It is a community of those—all of us—who share the prospect of a withdrawal from community that is, at once, a withdrawal of community. At the very heart of the community of mortals lies the exigency of this double withdrawal. The very sense of this community is that each and every member is subject to eventual withdrawal; it is a community based on the very withdrawal from/of community, a community that bears within itself its coming dissolution, its own demise.

And yet, even from this contradiction of being and nonbeing, a bond extends to others; or rather, others extend their reach toward the deceased, drawing him back, in a certain way, into being, resurrecting him. In memory and in all the forms in which memory can be objectified, in all the memorials that can be observed, and in all the monuments in which memory can be embodied, the deceased is brought back, is granted survival beyond death; in his very nonbeing, he is made present. For the most part, those who memorialize the deceased are the members of a community to which the one who has died belonged. The community may be that of the immediate or extended family, of close friends, or of a wider circle of others who knew him. At the very minimum, all these have in common a relation of a specific kind to the deceased, as well as the sorrow that they share in their mourning. They may share, in addition, reanimating memories of actions and events that were significant in the life of the one who has now passed away. In being memorialized in his very nonbeing, the deceased is drawn into these communities. Of those who memorialize him, bringing back the one who has passed away, it can be said that all have in common the bestowal of this gift of survival, of living on even while being dead. To this extent they form a community, even if they have little else in common. This community may be of brief duration, except in the hearts of those to whom the deceased was most beloved. Communities not only embrace a certain circle of persons but also are bounded by a certain duration. They display both extension and temporality.

While the community of mortals does indeed bear within itself dissolution through the withdrawal of its members in death, this dissolution is complemented by the memorial resurrection of those who have died. On the basis of this complementarity, the community of mortals is, to an extent, stabilized and preserved. No seeds of unqualified destruction are to be found in it.

Although Gonzalo presents his commonwealth as being totally communal, he seems completely oblivious to the commonality of death; there is no reference to the fact that whatever commonalities might be included in a particular community, the one irrepressible commonality is that of mortality. It appears that in a community in which all have all in common and in which this idyllic life would thrive on the basis of nature's bounty, death would lie at the furthest extreme and would barely, if at all, enter into its constitution.

Yet, at this point it is as if the dramatic turn that is taken were Shakespeare's way of slyly exposing Gonzalo's thorough neglect of the threat of violence or death. As soon as Gonzalo has finished delivering his speeches, he is laughed at and mocked ("Long *live* Gonzalo!"—italics added) by the treacherous courtesans Sebastian and Antonio. Gonzalo then falls asleep, as does also the weary, distressed Alonso, king of Naples; the king is quite unaware that the intention of the two courtesans is to murder him so that Sebastian, who is his brother, can assume the crown. Antonio imagines the scene:

> Th' occasion speaks thee, and
> My strong imagination sees a crown
> Dropping upon thy head.[24]

As Sebastian is egged on by thieving Antonio, they draw their swords to kill the sleeping king and Gonzalo as well, only to be interrupted as Ariel arrives, his "music and song" awaking Gonzalo and alerting him to the mortal danger. Thus, at the very last moment, the king is pulled back from death.

More, on the other hand, does give some attention to the human relation to death, though he fails to take account of the implications of mortality for the constitution of the Utopian community. His consideration of death is framed within the context of a larger concern with virtue, which in turn, he explicitly locates in the area of ethics. He declares that the Utopians "define virtue as living

---

24. Shakespeare, *The Tempest*, 2.1.207–209.

according to nature" and regard it as conducive to happiness, which lies "in pleasure that is good and honorable."[25] Death is the point of passage from one's virtues and good deeds in this life to the rewards to be enjoyed after this life; or from
crimes committed in this life to the punishments in store in the afterlife. And yet,
though the principles prescribing that death is such a transition are considered
rational and are taken by the Utopians to apply to all in their community, they
are principles within the community, not principles that contribute to the very
constitution of the community.

For Nancy, death is the primary determinant—indeed the sole determinant—
of community. His most decisive statement is that community is "calibrated on
the death [*ordonnée à la mort*] of those whom we call, perhaps wrongly, its members."[26] This determination of death stands in sharp contrast to Gonzalo's description of community: whereas Gonzalo's commonwealth is compact with commonality, which determines every aspect of the community, Nancy recognizes only
mortal community, that is, community that, as such, is determined by—calibrated
on—death. In More's *Utopia*, death is an event within the community, and in its
connection with virtue, it has ethical significance; yet, it does not in any manner determine community as such. Like Gonzalo's commonwealth, the Utopian
community is a site of total, if more moderate, commonality in which everything
belongs to everyone; it is a community in which this commonality binds together
all those who belong to the community.

What is at stake in Nancy's declaration that community is calibrated on death
is the manner in which the death of its members attests to the continual breach
of any community into which these (improperly called) members would be absorbed into a common substance, in which they would be fused into a seemingly
undisturbable community not entirely unlike that of Gonzalo. Nancy writes:
"The motif of the revelation, through death, of being-together or being-with, and
of the crystallization of the community around the death of its members, *that is
to say, around the 'loss' (the impossibility) of their immanence* and not around their
fusional assumption in some collective hypostasis, leads to a space of thinking in-
commensurable with the problematics of sociality and intersubjectivity (including the Husserlian problematic of the alter ego) within which philosophy, despite
its resistance, has remained captive."[27] In other words, death will always shatter
the totalized or purely immanent community, such that "death is indissociable,
for it is through death that the community reveals itself—and reciprocally."[28]
Yet, it is not only the death of the one who dies that is requisite for community;

25. More, *Utopia*, 82.
26. Jean-Luc Nancy, *La Communauté désoeuvrée* (Paris: Christian Bourgois, 1990), 41. First published in 1986.
27. Ibid., 39–40.
28. Ibid., 39.

rather, the community must be such that there reigns throughout—though there is no throughout—resistance to fusion in a common substance—whether it be the state, the church, or some other self-enclosed, purely immanent order.

In other words, what is at stake is a dying away from every such form of immanence. The result of this dying away from the life of immanence would be, in Blanchot's words, a community that "always posits the *absence* of community"; or, as Bataille terms it, a "community of those who do not have a community."[29] Nancy himself says much the same: it would be "a community that in a sense is without community." He continues: "Community without community is *to come*, in the sense that it is always *coming*, endlessly, at the heart of every collectivity."[30]

In Nancy's delimitation of community, two interrelated moments can be discerned. The first concerns death in its proper sense: the death of any member of a would-be community indeed attests to its instability; yet, it is not self-evident that the continual death of some—and for that matter, the birth of others—renders the community impossible. There is, to be sure, a continual shift, but such a process could be regarded as rendering community impossible only if community were construed as an absolutely static whole. But is every community that is other than a community without community constituted as pure immanence, as a fusing into an undisturbable unity all who belong to it, depriving them entirely of their singularity? While indeed there may be forces that aim at such repression of singularity, are there not also forces—and political action—that counter those of repression?

The second moment consists in withdrawal from immanence, from every collectivity, from all fusion into a common substance. What is decisive here is the distinctive difference between the determination of death in the two moments: while in the first moment, it is death proper, the death of singular persons, on which is calibrated the community without community; in the second moment, it is the *dying away* from immanence, from collectivity, that is at issue. The second moment, this *dying away*, does not directly calibrate a community, but, to the extent that it does so, it carries this out only *by analogy*. Dying away, that is, detaching oneself from a collectivity, is not to die.

The question remains: Do the deaths of singular persons bring about an unworking of community, a detaching of community from itself, the birth of a community without community? Or cannot opposition to a community that would absorb all persons into an unbreachable commonality take the form of active resistance, as with the political protests that, not without success, have challenged authoritarian regimes? Is such resistance dependent on withdrawal, or does it not

29. Maurice Blanchot, *La Communauté inavouable* (Paris: Les Éditions de Minuit, 1983), 9, 12.
30. Nancy, *La Communauté désoeuvrée*, 177.

require that one remain within the community in which one actively resists total-izing and repressive regimes that threaten the community to which one belongs?

C. Accord

It is because death as elemental belongs to the propriety of the human that death bears constitutively on the formation of human community. Death is not merely a possibility beyond the human toward which the self comports itself, but rath-er, precisely as improper, as exceeding the self indefinitely, infinitely, it is also bound up with the self: this bond is woven by the interplay between attraction, imagination, and reflection. Bound in this manner to death, humans can band together in communities only if their association is calibrated on death, which is displayed by the engagement of the community with death, as when one who has died is memorialized and thereby is, even though dead, brought back into the liv-ing community. It is not just that humans belong to the community of mortals; rather, mortality, that manifold bond to death, belongs to their very propriety. Death is one's own, not simply because one must die alone, but because, while infinitely exceeding oneself, it inheres in one's ownmost being, yet not only as the exigency of withdrawal but also as subject to the possibility of being brought back, precisely as withdrawn, into the community in such a way as to stabilize the community and prevent it from simply withdrawing.

Yet, death is not the only proper elemental and hence not the only binding element that, bearing on the self's constitution, is instrumental in determining the shape of human communities. For birth is no less decisive than death. One finds oneself there in the midst of life; one comes upon oneself as having been born, as bound to one's natality. As in the case of death, this bond is formed by the interplay of attraction, imagination, and reflection, though these often oper-ate only covertly. One is drawn back palintropically, returning in memory to-ward one's birth until, reaching the indefinite limit of one's memory, imagination comes into play to span the gap; as thus bound to one's birth, one is given back disclosively to oneself as having always already belonged to a community. One is given to understand oneself as having been born into a community, initially into the family (or its surrogate) as the primary community but also in a way that portends engagement in broader communities.

In having been born into a community, finding oneself there in its midst, one bears a complex of bequests: among these are certain beliefs, certain styles of behav-ior, certain types of action, and a particular language (sometimes more than one). Even if, as one develops a critical sense, one turns against certain of these bequests, the distancing from them will seldom lose all traces of them; only in the most excep-tional cases does one's voice cease to bear a trace of the mother tongue (and even of a particular dialect) into which—as the expression suggests—one will have been born.

The constitutive moments of community, its elemental conditions, extend beyond mortality and natality. Humans belong to nature, not only because they are surrounded by natural things, but also because nature exceeds the human, most powerfully in its elemental forms, and conveys to humans an understanding of themselves as engaged—perhaps unknowingly—in a constant and delicate exchange with nature. A community must be situated within a space in which this exchange can be freely carried on, that is, at a site where the interplay can eventuate between the human experience of nature and the reflection of nature back upon the human, disclosing both the place of the human in nature and nature itself in its force and in its beauty.

It belongs to community that there occurs in it various interlacings of beliefs, of intentions, and in this connection there are also disagreements, contention, and aggression. In all these kinds of comportment, there is the possibility—and no doubt often the occurrence—of concealment, that is, various forms of seclusion. The expression of an intention can always serve to hide a person's actual intention. Concealment of the same sort is possible in the case of beliefs, a confession of certain beliefs being put forth to hide a person's actual beliefs and to allow this person thereby to deceive others. In disagreements and in contention or aggressive behavior, it is seldom clear what all the pertinent issues are and what, behind the scenes, motivates such behavior.

The most powerful form of seclusion is that indigenous to embodiment. The body constitutes a limit to the clarity of the in-common; it is a dimension of the human that resists community while, at once, belonging inescapably to it. This peculiar disconnection between community and embodiment is expressed most succinctly in the *Republic*. In the course of prescribing the requisite way of life of the guardians of the πόλις, Socrates stipulates that they are to be deprived of all private possessions so as to have everything in common, hence forming a community of the most extreme kind. Yet, he observes that the one possession of which they cannot be deprived is their body. Thus, Socrates speaks of "their possessing nothing private except the body, while all other things are held in common."[31] The body resists inclusion in the community and yet is inseparable from all that belongs to it. The body adheres to the community yet withdraws from the in-common. As seclusion it is an outside coiled within the inside; it is darkness in the midst of light.

Community as experienced in modernity has been identified with space itself, with the spacing of the outside-of-self.[32] This identification is suggestive in that the self that occupies the space of community is precisely a self outside of

---

31. Plato, *Republic* 464d.
32. Nancy, *La Communauté désoeuvrée*, 50. Attributed to Bataille.

itself, not in the sense of being solely ecstatic, sheer ecstasy, but in the sense of having primary determinants of its propriety outside itself, indefinitely exceeding itself. The identification is also suggestive in that it posits a certain coincidence of community and space; and while it is not tenable to posit a simple identity between community and space, it must be acknowledged that a community is always in some respect spatially situated. And yet, to be precise, a community neither is space itself nor is it located in space itself, in space as such; for space purely as such or even as luminous lacks all articulation and differentiation and is entirely incapable of providing bounds within which community could take place. Rather, what is required is that the space, specifically the interspace bounded by the natural elementals, preeminently by earth and sky, be delimited into regions or places. What community coincides with—without effacing the difference—are delimited places, specifically determinate places on the surface of the earth. This bond between community and place is no merely abstract or general relation. Community literally takes place where, for example, rivers bring water, where the soil is fertile, where rain and sunshine enable the bounty of nature—all these occurrences within an articulated place making it possible, even desirable, for humans to abide there.

Thus, a community set in its articulated place is an abode. It is the abode one would reenter in the return from solitude. It is the abode to which one will always have advanced from one's proximal abode; for one is never entirely alone except in the necessarily limited intervals of solitude. Within the communal abode, one is already tacitly oriented to the political abode, in which communities are bound together by laws. Placed communally on the surface of the earth, one is already engaged with nature, with the natural elements, and beyond in imagination or through the dissolution of the sky by means of the instruments of post-Galilean astronomy. From the communal abode, one reaches out to all abodes; one engages, even if tacitly, with the entire nest of abodes.

Community is thus set within the compass of the two configurations that constitute ethicality, that of the proper elementals and that of the nest of abodes. As abiding in one's community, it is incumbent—is indeed an imperative—that one appropriate to one's full capacity the reflected elemental self-understanding as it bears on one's being-in-community and that one become ever more visionary in looking out beyond—yet from within—one's community. It is in this way that, as abiding in one's community, one enters into enhanced ethicality and at the same time furthers the ethical composure of one's community at large.

D. The Ethical

In community one is drawn into an expansiveness in which one can flourish in uncountable ways. From the elementals as they enter into the constitution of community, there comes a draft that draws the self beyond to an enhanced self-understanding. In community one is drawn toward the other, and, above all, in love one wins oneself, one gains oneself in intense passion. The self is drawn into a more acute vision beyond, toward the political, nature, and the cosmos; this draft entices one to become more visionary. In the prospect that death will be complemented by memorialization, the self is drawn into the hope and promise of living on.

In community there eventuates, not an ethical demand, but an ethical draft; to enter into this draft, to station oneself in the gentle gale, is to broach the promise of enhancements of one's life. It is this promise that may appropriately be called *the ethical*.

The defining principle of community is commonality, that is, having in common. If this principle is taken without qualification or limitation, then it prescribes that in a community all are to have all in common. And yet, there are decisive indications that limitation must be applied to this principle, that each term must be rethought and redetermined. Perhaps nothing demonstrates the untenability of the bare principle more graphically than Gonzalo's presentation of a community based on this principle in completely unqualified form; in addition to its utterly unreliable dependence on nature, on nature's free and equal distribution of all to all, the structure of this community ends up recoiling on itself in a stark contradiction. Furthermore, the example of Plato's guardians underlines the limitation to which the principle is subject in the fact of human embodiment. Still further, though More's Utopia is based on this same ungarnished form of the principle, even if with a certain moderation, More himself, in his initial exchange with his fictitious narrator, raises strong objections to the conception of commonality based on the principle in unqualified form. To the narrator's assertion that such a community alleviates many ills, More responds: "Quite the contrary, it seems to me that no one can live comfortably where everything is held in common. For how can there be any abundance of goods when everyone stops working because he is no longer motivated by making a profit, and grows lazy because he relies on the labors of others."[33] Even after he has heard the report on the Utopians' community, More's doubts are not allayed: "When Raphael had ended his tale, there occurred to me quite a few institutions established by the customs and laws of that nation which seemed to me quite absurd, not only in their way of waging war, their religious beliefs and practices, and other institutions as well, but also (and above all) in the very point that is the principal foundation of their whole social structure, namely their common life and subsistence with no exchange of money."[34]

---

33. More, *Utopia*, 48.
34. Ibid., 134.

In order for there to be community, there must be something in common to all who belong to the community; they must share something. It would not, then, be a matter of *having* something, not a matter of possessing it, not even of extensive joint possession. The question as to what form of possession is appropriate is thus irrelevant. Whether there is private property or not has nothing to do with community; for one can share with others what is one's own as well as what is not privately owned by anyone and lies, for example, in the public sphere. No individual owns the city park, but one can share it with others.

The ethical eventuates as a call on one to share with those in one's community without any predetermined limit to qualify the sharing; its extent and its form in each situation depends largely on the reciprocal engagement that one enjoys with others. One's response to the call may be an opening for sharing, and what is to be shared, above all, are the innumerable ethical drafts that promise to draw others in the community into an enhancement of life. On the other hand, the bearing of the ethical can be interrupted by deceptive, contentious, or aggressive postures or actions within the community. The sharing can also be limited by occasions of withdrawal if, as Arendt maintains, there is need for a place where one can find protection from "the light of publicity."[35] There can also be limitation from above, especially when there is an incursion of the political into the community.

* * *

The call of the ethical may be lent the voice of the poet; it may be echoed in song. It may be sung for all humanity, beckoning to all humans gathered together as a single great community. The austere, monotonous silence of the community of the dying would be broken by a joyful hymn to life proclaiming that *alle Menschen werden Brüder.*

---

35. Arendt links this need to private property: "The only efficient way to guarantee the darkness of what needs to be hidden against the light of publicity is private property, a privately owned place to hide in." Hannah Arendt, *The Human Condition*, 71. Yet, there are other places where one can, if only for a limited time, escape the light of publicity, for example, in the wilderness.

5   Governance

A. The Onset of Politics

In the beginning there was no politics, no need of politics. It was as in Gonzalo's commonwealth, in which all that might precipitate strife was excluded and the necessities of life were provided by nature with such abundance that nothing occasioned private possession nor any of the oppositions or conflicts that would require governance.

The beginning shone like gold. It was in the time when Cronos ruled that the gods created the "golden race of mortals."[1] They lived without toil, for the bounteous earth bore them abundant fruit. They dwelled in peace beyond the reach of evil and were loved by the gods.

But then everything was reversed. Cronos was dethroned by his son, and the age of Zeus commenced. Those of the silver race, which the gods now created, were unable in their foolishness to refrain from violence against one another and from neglect of sacrifice, which angered the gods. Opposition, strife, was as rampant among them as peace had been for the golden race. Only a reconciling governance, only an onset of politics, could have saved them from the destruction they suffered at the hands of Zeus.

The Stranger calls it a great myth (μεγάλος μῦθος). It is launched as a new beginning (ἀρχή), following the image of dialectical divisions that has, up to that point, been the sole preoccupation in the *Statesman*. It is a palintropic beginning that turns back in order to mark the beginning of the present era. It describes a golden age from which the present age developed, or rather, departed, by a complete reversal. From the age of the rule of Cronos the reversal led to the unruliness of the age of Zeus.

The Stranger describes how the reversal came about. This description forms the very heart of the great myth: "During a certain time the god himself goes with the universe, conducting it in its revolving course, and at another time, when the cycles have at length reached the measure of the allotted time, he lets it go and of its own accord [or: spontaneously—αὐτόματον] it turns backward in the opposite direction."[2] It is at this time, when the god turns it loose and the universe then

---

1. Hesiod, *Works and Days*, 109–10.
2. Plato, *Statesman* 269c–d. All the citations in the following discussion of the *Statesman* are taken from sections 271e–274d.

moves of its own accord, that politics begins. It is precisely the word αὐτόματον that expresses the consequent necessity of politics.

As if to stress the inevitability of the recurrence of such reversals, the Stranger sets about describing, not the changeover *from* the age of Cronos to the present age of Zeus, but rather the passage *to* the age of Cronos from a previous age that, though not identified as such, seems entirely like the present age. It is in this reversal of the reversal—as if he were describing a transition from the present age back to the previous one—that the Stranger situates his account. He explains that as a result of this transition (back) to the age of Cronos, mortal beings ceased to age and instead began to grow younger. The white hair of old men turned black and their beards disappeared. The young men became smaller day by day until, having become like newborn children, they withered away and disappeared completely. At the opposite extreme, those who were dead and lay in the earth were born out of the earth. Not only was the order of birth and death reversed but also for this reason there was no procreation and presumably no ἔρως; there were, says the Stranger, "no possessions of women and children." Moreover, it was inevitable that with any reversal of the revolution of the cosmos, the course of human life would also undergo a reversal; for time itself, as shown in the *Timaeus*,[3] is linked to—indeed is nothing other than—the movement of the cosmos, so that a reversal of cosmic movements is, *a fortiori*, a reversal of time itself, hence also of the temporal course of human life.

In the age of Cronos, sovereignty belonged solely to the gods. The Stranger explains: "At that time, the god who had it [the cosmos] in his care first ruled the circling itself as a whole, and likewise in region by region there was this same kind of rule, when all the parts of the cosmos had been distributed under ruling gods." The divine shepherds grazed all animals, so that there were none that were savage or that consumed one another. Also, "there was no war at all or sedition," for the gods also grazed humans just as humans shepherd their flocks. Thus—most decisively—under this divine sovereignty there were no πόλεις: "when the god was grazing [humans], there were no regimes [πολιτεῖαι]." As long as the gods ruled, there was no need of politics.

But then Cronos turned loose, let go of the cosmos, as he and all the other gods withdrew from exercising sovereignty over all living beings. This deed and the reversal it produced coincided with another event, which the Stranger describes in these words: "When each soul had fulfilled all its births, as it had let fall into the earth as many seeds as had been prescribed for each, it was precisely at that moment that the helmsman of the universe, just as if he had let go

---

3. Plato, *Timaeus* 37d. See my analysis of this passage in *Chorology: On Beginning in Plato's "Timaeus"* (Bloomington: Indiana University Press, 1999), 77–85.

of the handle of the rudder, stood apart and withdrew to his place of outlook [περιωπή]." Once the god had withdrawn, the beasts became savage and were a mortal threat to humans, who were saved from extermination only by the generous gifts from the gods, the gifts of fire, τέχνη, and seeds and plants. In the present age of Zeus in which all the gods—and indeed Zeus himself—remain withdrawn and, except for these gifts that assured the survival of humans, withhold their care, humans have "to manage their way of life and their own care for themselves." It is when human action begins to take place of its own accord, when humans must determine their deeds by themselves, spontaneously, rather than as prescribed by the gods, when they confront the necessity to act αὐτόματον—it is then that politics commences.

Precisely because of the character of the present age of Zeus, the Stranger abandons the conception of the sovereign as the shepherd of the human herd; for this conception implies that for those thus shepherded there is no need to act on their own and hence no need of politics. Contrary to this conception, the Stranger determines the character that the statesman must possess in the present age of Zeus by reference to the paradigm of weaving: the statesman is the one whose duty is to weave together such τέχναι as that of the general and that of the judge; as caring in this manner for *all* things in the πόλις, the statesman is himself distinct from all these concerns, and his power is properly designated as politics (πολιτική). In this capacity he no longer imitates the gods as shepherding humans but rather rules in a way that is appropriate to a time in which humans must act on their own, αὐτόματον. As soon as each acts on his own, as soon as each determines his acts spontaneously, by himself, differences will be inevitable and conflicts will erupt; a means of mediating and moderating these becomes indispensable. Then it is imperative that there be an onset of politics.

In the *Republic* the onset of politics is represented by depiction of the role that τέχνη plays in the development of the πόλις that Socrates, Glaucon, and Adeimantus undertake to build in λόγος. Although no such connection is even alluded to in either dialogue, this account may be regarded as taking up the description of the emergence of politics at the point where, in the *Statesman*, the gods withdrew and extended to humans nothing further except the τέχναι, the fire required for many forms of τέχνη, and the seeds and plants necessary for sustenance.

The first in the series of πόλεις that are built consists simply of artisans practicing the basic τέχναι by which to provide the primary needs for food, housing, and clothing. Socrates specifies that each artisan should practice only the τέχνη for which he is naturally suited—"one man, one τέχνη," as Adeimantus puts it.[4]

---

4. Plato, *Republic* 370b. In the immediately following discussion, the unreferenced citations are taken from *Republic* 370b–373d.

Socrates observes that in order to satisfy basic needs, a πόλις would require a farmer, a house builder, and a weaver, and perhaps a shoemaker or some other man providing things for the body. Thus, the most basic πόλις, one capable of satisfying the need for such things as food, housing, and clothing, "would consist of four or five men." In this description there is no mention of any need for governance, for someone who would oversee the practice of the necessary τέχναι. Rather, each artisan would—without any compulsion—produce enough for both his own needs and the needs of the other three or four artisans. So, with each producing enough for all and freely exchanging with the others, there would prevail a kind of natural harmony.

Yet, the πόλις will rapidly expand beyond this tiny group of artisans. There is need for someone to make the farmer's plow and another to produce the tools that will allow the house builder, the weaver, and the shoemaker to carry on their work. Still others will be needed—smiths, herdsmen, merchants, tradesmen— though these additions do not alter the primary purpose of providing for the basic needs of the citizens; neither would they disturb the natural harmony between these artisans, each providing both for himself and for all others in need of his products or services. Their way of life will be peaceful, healthy, and pleasant: "Setting out noble loaves of barley and wheat on some reeds or clean leaves, they will stretch out on rushes strewn with yew and myrtle and feast themselves and their children. Afterwards they will drink wine and, crowned with wreathes, sing of the gods." They will have no need of politics.

And yet, Glaucon strongly objects to such a way of life "without relishes" and abruptly declares that this is a πόλις of pigs! He could hardly have interjected a more insulting reference: the Greeks regarded pigs as very lowly, despicable creatures that were dirty and stupid and would eat the most disgusting things. So, Socrates, now joined by Glaucon, sets out to build a second πόλις in which there will be all kinds of refinements and luxuries. This luxurious πόλις will be gorged with all sorts of things that are not necessary, that do not satisfy any basic needs. Desire will soon outdistance supply, and as a result they must "cut off a piece of [their] neighbor's land." For this purpose an army is required, or rather, a corp of men skilled in military τέχνη. Thus are guardians (φυλακή) introduced into the πόλις, and though their superior status only gradually becomes explicit in the discussion, it can be observed in the fact that, from this point on, the discussion largely concerns only the guardians; it is as though all the other, more ordinary artisans simply stick to their τέχναι and enjoy the pleasures of the luxurious πόλις.

With the introduction of this division within the πόλις, with the installation of the superior class of guardians charged with protecting the artisans at large, an incipient politics comes into view. It becomes more prominent as, along with a series of purges of the luxurious πόλις, the principle governing the artisans (one man, one τέχνη) is extended to include also the prescription that each man is to be strictly bound to the practice of his τέχνη, that this is to be his sole and constant engagement, that he is not to be distracted by the pleasures offered by the luxurious πόλις,[5] The entire life of the artisans comes to be ruled. The stage is thus set for the introduction of the distinction that is most decisive in determining the onset of politics in the πόλις: Socrates distinguishes among the guardians between auxiliaries (ἐπίκουρος), who are the warriors and protectors of the πόλις, and the rulers (ἄρχων).[6] When Glaucon later offers an image that is descriptive of this differentiation—namely, "we put the auxiliaries in our πόλις like dogs obedient to the rulers, who are like shepherds of a πόλις"[7]—it is almost as if the discourse in the *Statesman* about the divine shepherds grazing their human flocks had been renewed. At this point the politics of the πόλις built in λόγος has become full blown.

And yet, still further, in the course of the great detour through philosophy, which commences at the beginning of Book 5 and runs to the beginning of Book 8, the discourse converges still more sharply toward that of the *Statesman*. For it turns out that from among the rulers there is to be one who is the sole ruler proper. This ruler is to be either a philosopher who has become also a ruler or a ruler who has become also a philosopher. Moreover, his ascendancy bears comparison with the withdrawal of the god: as the god let go of the cosmos and withdrew outside it to a place offering a superior view (περιωπή), so the philosopher-ruler exits the cave—that is, the πόλις—and withdraws to an upper region where he, too, is offered a superior view—of things in their truth. He is to the πόλις what the god is to the cosmos; and just as the god will return to the cosmos, again taking hold and launching a new age, so the philosopher-ruler will return to the cave-πόλις, bringing his gift of order and rule, reversing the disorder, the unruliness, and the ignorance that had reigned there.

But how, within the πόλις, does the sovereign exercise his rule? The *Statesman* offers a specific account. Once the god has withdrawn, ruling can no longer consist in shepherding the flock of humans. Once the cosmos begins to turn in the opposite direction, enormous disruptions break out: humans are caught up in the wildness, the violence, the threatening forces and fierce beasts, as well as, within themselves, the conflicts wrought by erotic passions; they are no longer the tame, placid, obedient animals they were when shepherded by the god. Now they require means such as τέχνη in order to provide for and protect themselves, and, in ruling, the statesman cares for all these things in the πόλις and "weaves

---

5. See Ibid., 421a.
6. See Ibid., 414b.
7. Ibid., 440a.

them together most correctly."[8] The statesman thus reverses the course set when the god let go of the cosmos, that is, he reverses the reversal—as the philosopher-ruler, returning to the cave, sets about reversing the disarray and ignorance that had prevailed there.

At the very end of the *Statesman*, the metaphor of weaving is again put in play, but now in a figure that both refines and expands the earlier description. The Stranger identifies the two dominant moments or virtues that are inherent in human action and, correspondingly, form the poles in the life of the πόλις. These two moments, courage (ἀνδρεία) and moderation (σωφροσύνη), both taken in the very broadest sense, form the warp and woof of the statesman's weaving. The statesman weaves them into "the best and most magnificent of all webs"[9] and then wraps everyone else in the πόλις in this beautifully woven fabric.

B. Double Visage

The statesman is Janus-faced.

Janus was the god of good beginnings, which, in turn, promised good endings. His temple in Rome ran east and west, from where the day begins to where it ends; he oversaw the two portals at the opposite ends of the temple, and his statue stood midway between them. He had two faces looking in opposite directions, one turned toward the east portal, toward sunrise, the other toward the west portal, toward sunset. The two portals were closed only when Rome was at peace.

The statesman[10] also launches beginnings. He has one face turned toward political possibilities, the other turned toward those whom he governs. They are good possibilities if they enhance the lives of those who are governed, that is, who abide in the polity.[11] The statesman also mediates, like Janus standing in the middle of his temple. He is both the one who envisages the political possibilities and the one who oversees their actualization, who double-faced, mediates between these possibilities and their actualization.

---

8. Plato, *Statesman* 305e.
9. Ibid., 311c.
10. In the present discourse, the Latin-based terms *statesman* and *sovereign* are used synonymously to designate a ruler. The word *statesman* is the common translation of the title of Plato's dialogue Πολιτικός. The word *Souveränität* is used in Hegel's *Philosophy of Right*, §§281, 282, 293. The Greek-derived term *politician* is avoided primarily because of its negative connotations; unfortunately this choice effaces the connection with πόλις. On the other hand, *statesman* and *sovereign* do not refer here only to an honorable ruler but are meant to designate a wide range of rulers.
11. The word *polity* derives from the Latin *politia*, which translates πολιτεία, derived, in turn, from πόλις. *Polity* was used in English writings as early as the sixteenth century to mean a civil order, civil organization, an organized society or state. In the present discourse, it is used to signify any type of civil organization, including city, state, and nation; it is also intended to refer back to πόλις and πολιτεία and hence to the Greek origin of politics as such.

This most rudimentary political structure is required if there is to be governance, which is the basic core of a polity. The one can be many, and even in democracy this structure is retained, though in thoroughly reduced form. On the other hand, to determine the shape of a community and hence of a polity by reference solely to death, to a dying away from community, which results in the conception of a community without community, cannot suffice to formulate a determination of a polity. For a polity that would escape all immanence, that would be a polity without being a polity, that would lack even the barest political structure, would be no polity at all. Could the result be anything other than a chaos, an anarchy, in which the lives of those improperly called citizens would be drained of all vital possibilities?

It is the charge of the statesman—one, many, or all—to envision good political possibilities, that is, possibilities that, to a large extent, are beneficial. Others are charged with actualizing certain of the possibilities that have been envisioned, namely, those that are determined as good, as displaying the capacity to enhance the lives of the citizens.

At a more originary level, the envisioned possibilities are grounded in submission to ethicality. For the reversion from ethicality grants a certain self-understanding, an intensification of the self's reflection upon itself. Yet, in order for the ethical self-understanding to expand into political understanding, the self must pass through a mutation[12] in which the self's reflection upon itself is reconstituted as a reflective circuit in which the self turns beyond itself to others; in other words, the reflective circuit in which the self turns upon itself, mutates into a reflective circuit in which, without relinquishing its selfhood, the self turns to others. In the political sphere, the others will consist of those who share such formative factors as custom, law, and various institutions. The effect of this mutation is to extend the ethical self-understanding to a political understanding in the form of the envisioning of possibilities.

Possibilities cannot be envisioned by sense. They are not simply there before the perceptually oriented self; they are not accessible to the senses. Neither are they merely semantic correlates, only to be said without any concrete connection to things and the prospect of actualization amidst things. It is only in and through imagination that possibilities can be envisioned, can be brought forth.

It is precisely such imaginative envisionment that is all too often lacking, not least of all in recent times. In place of an imaginative prospect of decisions to come, only the most routine and sedimented alternatives come into consideration and figure in decisions, most pervasively when they are essentially political. Rather than possibilities being envisioned that exceed the measure of the present,

---

12. On mutations, see chap. 3, section B.

the future is planned, and its course is predicted on the basis of mere calculation and extrapolation from the present. Such methods and the plans deriving from them merely repeat in various guises—and without renewal—the well-worn possibilities of the past rather than opening a prospect for the future, offering promise and hope as well as protraction of danger. For the future is absolute possibility and absolute danger.

Possibilities are not images, and imagination is not primarily a power of entertaining images, neither phantastical images composed from things once seen, nor images of sensible objects no longer seen. Rather, imagination is tractive, a power of drawing forth prospects that would otherwise remain veiled. Not only are possibilities drawn forth by imagination but also they are determined by an orientation toward actualization, not toward any particular actualizations, but toward actualization as such. A possibility is a prospect (*prospicere*) in that it simulates a looking ahead toward actualization.

Imagination has the capacity to peer through the veil that covers hitherto undisclosed possibilities and to draw the veil aside so as to draw these possibilities into its sphere. And yet, there are possibilities (to the extent that the copula is appropriate) that are more remote, that fall indefinitely outside the compass of those that are merely veiled, possibilities whose veil is itself veiled, possibilities that lie beyond the limits that measure the domain of the merely veiled. This is the connection in relation to which to read the words of Rousseau: "It is imagination that extends for us the measure of the possible."[13]

Whereas imagination brings forth possibilities, it does not determine whether these are *good* possibilities and whether therefore it is desirable, in a proper setting with appropriate customs—that is, granted a certain ἦθος—that they be actualized. For such a determination, judgment is required, not judgment in a purely formal sense, but as based on a certain content. In order to judge whether a certain possibility is good, whether goodness can be attributed to it, one must

---

13. Jean-Jacques Rousseau, *Emile: Or On Education*, trans. Allan Bloom (New York: Basic Books, 1979), 81. Originally published in 1762, almost simultaneously with the *Social Contract*. Despite the accomplishment that Rousseau attributes to imagination, he regards it as leading humans beyond the natural state in which power and desire are in equilibrium. Thus, to the statement just cited, he adds: "whether for good or bad, and which consequently excites and nourishes the desires by the hope of satisfying them. But the object which at first appeared to be at hand flees more quickly than it can be pursued." Consequently, such a pursuit of happiness spurred on by imagination is doomed to failure. And yet, another passage in *Emile* advises the teacher how to help a young man avert the danger of imagination: "Do not stifle his imagination; guide it lest it engender monsters" (325). Still another passage focuses on the enjoyment that imagination can produce: "Imagination joins to the spectacle of spring that of the seasons that are going to follow it. To these tender buds that the eye perceives, imagination adds the flowers, the fruits, the shadows, and sometimes the mysteries they can cover. It concentrates in a single moment the times that are going to follow one another" (158).

understand, however tacitly, that the good consists in self-enhancement, in an expansion of the sense of self, in the disclosure of a hitherto unrecognized receptivity or creativeness. By means of imagination accompanied by judgment, the horizon of one's vision in the broad sense may be extended; or one's spirit may be more finely attuned to the beauty of nature and art or prepared for a more profound engagement with others.

The possibilities that are envisioned can be effective only if they are actualized either by the statesman himself (weaving various strands together) or by other citizens (using more common means). Once they are actualized, the possibilities, which were previously only imagined, take on visible or audible form; the imagined possibilities are objectified. The relation between the one who envisions a possibility and the one (perhaps even the same one) who actualizes it can vary from complete accord, in which the possibility is truly objectified, to such discord as erupts if the object distorts the possibility or if the possibility presented for actualization proves intrinsically incapable of being truly fabricated. These two extremes can be regarded as forms of civil justice and injustice, respectively.

* * *

The imperative to which the statesman is bound requires that he envision good political possibilities. Such possibilities are those that enhance the lives of those governed by the statesman. Yet, how such enhancement is brought about differs from one polity to another, depending on the location, character, and customs of each polity, on their ἦθος. Nonetheless, there are certain overreaching requirements that must be met in order for a set of political possibilities to be determined as good, and likewise, for the polities in which these possibilities are actual. Foremost among these requirements is concordance with ethicality.

There is special accord between the political abode, on the one hand, and the abodes of nature and community. Since these two abodes are adjacent to the political abode, the spiraling between the three abodes is prominent, as is their accordance. Any polity as such sustains an adherence to nature and to community.

Since all humans not only belong to nature, on which they are inescapably dependent, but also have nature incorporated into themselves in the form of the body, the sense of self gives one both an orientation to nature and a concern, however underdeveloped, for the care of nature. A good political possibility in this regard, one bearing enhancement of the natural dimension of one's life, would prescribe means by which the nature in and around humans would be granted the care and respect that the human sense of self indicates for it, means such as instilling such comportments in citizens by education or by adopting appropriate legislation. Needless to say, there are all too many cases in which this common good has been inverted into exploitation of nature. This inversion is exemplified in Marx's overt ambivalence. On the one hand, he says of man that "he is nature." Or again: "*Man* is directly a *natural* being . . . endowed with *natural powers of life*."[14] On the other hand, Marx presides over what he regards as the dissolution of nature. In his criticism of Feuerbach in *The German Ideology*, he writes that "the sensuous world around him," that is, nature, is "the product of industry and the state of society . . .; it is an historical product, the result of the activity of a whole succession of generations."[15] Or again, in *Capital*: "Thus nature becomes one of the organs of his [the laborer's] activity, one that he annexes to his own bodily organs."[16]

And yet, today one cannot but be acutely aware of the consequences—as in Eastern Europe—of the exploitation of nature. One of the most devastating effects is the destruction of the natural habitats of many animal species, as, for instance, the destruction of forests by the logging industry, which threatens many forest-dwelling animals such as deer, squirrels, woodchucks, and more. The result has been to drive many species, those that are less adaptable, to the threshold—or beyond—of extinction.

Arendt, on the other hand, though alluding to Marx, takes a different stance and looks upon nature through a different lens. She writes: "While nature manifests itself in human existence through the circular movement of our bodily functions, she makes her presence felt in the man-made world through the constant threat of overgrowing or decaying it."[17] Thus, for Arendt, it is a matter of protection against the threat of nature rather than its dissolution that is to be undertaken. Nature, it seems, is a kind of enemy that has to be kept at bay, since otherwise it will overrun the human world. What is needed is mastery of nature and a politics that would enforce it.

And yet, it has become clear beyond all doubt that nature cannot be kept at bay outside the walls of the polity. For today, exposed to virtually unlimited exploitation or engaged as an enemy to be kept under control, nature returns from its destitution. It returns in a guise other than that which is regarded as natural for nature, as its proper guise—sometimes as utterly disfigured, sometimes as amplified to monstrous proportions. When wildfires consume enormous areas of forests, when hurricanes threaten and sometimes destroy coastal cities with ever greater frequency, when glaciers, which have been intact for ages, begin to melt, threatening worldwide ocean levels, the return of nature in destructive guise is

---

14. Karl Marx, *Economic and Philosophic Manuscripts of 1844*, trans. Martin Milligan (Amherst, NY: Prometheus Books, 1988), 154. First published in 1930.
15. Karl Marx and Friedrich Engels, *The German Ideology* (Mansfield Centre, CT: Martino Publishing, 1939), 35. First published in 1932.
16. Karl Marx, *Capital*, vol. 1, *Critical Analysis of Capitalist Production*, ed. Friedrich Engels (New York: International Publishers, 1967), 179. First published in 1867.
17. Hannah Arendt, *The Human Condition*, 98.

manifest to such an extent that one can only despair that there is so little effective political response operative.

The abode of community bears also on that of politics, since both have the capacity to provide a place in which are enhanced the lives of those who abide in the community or in the polity. Thus, each represents an actualization of a good political possibility on a lesser and a greater scale. Just as humans are bound to nature and with only rare exceptions belong to a polity, so there are virtually none who do not to some degree abide in a community into which they will have been born and by which they may be memorialized after their death. However strenuously one may have detached oneself, there remain, almost without exception, traces of one's natal community.

Within a polity in which various communities are assembled, one may be led to communicate across the lines separating one's community from others, drawing oneself temporarily into that other community, while remaining no less within one's own community. The event is one of being outside oneself, which is possible only if one also remains oneself. Since in this event one is, for a brief time, both oneself and empathetically an other, the effect can be to undermine prejudice.

And yet, prejudice and its ill effects pale by comparison with a wholly corrupt political system.

What should provide enhancement of the lives of those abiding in a polity can be corrupted so as to serve only the interests of a single powerful person. Such a person represents the total degradation of the statesman and the utter corruption of politics. His actions, invariably oriented to gaining and retaining power, violate the very sense of statesmanship. The tyrant typically conceals his power and his villainy behind a wall of disguises and lies. He employs various means not only to hide his plotting from "the masses" but also to distract them from detecting the real state of affairs. Uncontrolled consumption ("bread and circuses") may be promoted as the means to happiness. Genuine political discourse is replaced with empty slogans—all this and more while the tyrant feigns great concern for the welfare of the populace and dismisses the efforts of those who might expose him. In the most dismal cases, he resorts to exile or murder.

There is no more penetrating depiction of the tyrant than that expressed by Socrates in the *Republic*. The tyrant represents the final stage in the decline of the πόλις. Central to Socrates's description is the role played by ἔρως in its most corrupt and distorted form.

Socrates explains that the process begins when the soon-to-be tyrant wanders from the noble opinions he had received as a child and gives himself over to opinions that foster robbery, violation of temples, and other such wicked deeds. The decline into tyranny has then been prepared: "These are the opinions that were formerly released as dreams in sleep when, still under laws and a father, there was a democratic regime in him. But once a tyranny was established by ἔρως, what he had rarely been in dreams, he became continuously while awake. He will stop at no terrible murder, or food, or deed. Rather, ἔρως lives like a tyrant within him in all anarchy and lawlessness; and being a monarch, will lead the man whom it controls, as though he were a πόλις, to every kind of daring" that will produce wherewithal for it and the noisy crowd around it.[18]

Machiavelli's prince is not simply a tyrant. Though there are indeed princes who commit tyrannical deeds, the actions of most princes lie somewhere between those of a tyrant and those of a statesman. There are those who have become princes through the most shameful wickedness. Machiavelli cites the example of Agathocles the Sicilian, whose heinous deed was a result of his determination to hold onto the position to which he had risen in Sicilian politics and to execute all who might stand in his way: "one morning he called together the people and the senate of Syracuse as if he were going to discuss some matters concerning the republic. At a prearranged signal he had his troops kill all the senators and the richest citizens; and when they were dead, he seized and held the rule of the city without any opposition from the citizenry."[19] Among the true statesmen, Machiavelli mentions Francesco Sforza, who "became Duke of Milan from his station as a private citizen through appropriate methods and a great deal of virtue and . . . with a thousand hardships"; and Cesare Borgia, who "did everything and used every method that a prudent and virtuous man ought to employ."[20]

The Prince must be read from the end, from the exhortation that constitutes the final chapter. The exhortation is a summons to free Italy from the "foreign floods" of barbarians, who by military and political means, dominate the disunited states of Italy from Milan in the north to Naples in the south. Those whom Machiavelli brands as barbarians are in fact the Swiss, the Spanish, the Germans, and above all, the French. The exhortation expresses also the hope of uniting Italy and at the same time an awareness of the present condition of Italy as "without a leader, without order, beaten, despoiled, ripped apart, overrun, and having suffered every sort of ruin."[21] The exhortation calls for an inversion of this miserable condition; it appeals to "Your Illustrious House" and specifies this appeal in the book's dedication to the Magnificent Lorenzo de' Medici. Though in 1513 when Machiavelli wrote *The Prince*, there was a Medici pope (Leo X) and Medici princes in control of Florence, and grounds for hope that they would form a strong unifying state and banish the foreigners, this hope was dashed when, in

18. Plato, *Republic* 574d–575a.
19. Niccolò Machiavelli, *The Prince*, trans. Peter Bondanella (Oxford: Oxford University Press, 2005), chap. 8.
20. Ibid., chap. 7.
21. Ibid., chap. 26.

1519, both Leo X and Lorenzo de' Medici died. The possibility of the transformation called for in the exhortation was greatly diminished.

The Prince is addressed not only to princes and those who desire to become princes but also to their subjects, to the citizens. In *The Social Contract* Rousseau writes regarding Machiavelli: "While appearing to instruct kings, he has done much to educate the people."[22] Rousseau's words echo those of the eulogy of Machiavelli written in the sixteenth century by Alberico Gentili: "He was extremely hostile to tyranny. Therefore, he did not help the tyrant; his intention was not to instruct the tyrant but to make all his secrets clear and to display openly the degree of wretchedness to the people. . . . While appearing to instruct the prince, he was actually educating the people."[23] Thus, in connection with the exhortation, Machiavelli writes that in Italy "there is great virtue in the limbs, were it not for the lack of it in the heads"[24]—that is, the common mass of Italians have substantial capability, but Italy's leaders lack it. Thus, *The Prince* has a double aim, as attested by Machiavelli's remark that it is his "intention to write something useful for anyone who understands it."[25] Clearly his advice to princes can be useful; but it can also be useful to the citizens, since it enables them to recognize a situation in which the prince aims to keep them well disposed, as well as those in which the prince exploits and endangers them. So, on the one side, Machiavelli advises princes how to gain power and how to keep it. For the measures that he adopts, there is, he insists, no tribunal that, most consequentially, would ban cruelty. Yet, even cruelty is in order if it is necessary to assure the unity and stability of the state, that is, it is the political end that is decisive: "Therefore, a prince must not worry about the infamy of being considered cruel when it is a matter of keeping his subjects united and loyal. . . . Of all the types of princes, the new prince cannot escape the reputation for cruelty, since new states are full of dangers."[26] Yet, it is not only a matter of contending with dangers but also, in view of the exhortation, the exigency of forming princes whose virtue would enable them to take part in freeing and unifying Italy.

The priority of these goals is expressed by Hegel. *The Prince*, he observes

> is often taken to contain secrets of and maxims for despotism. If one reads particularly the conclusion of that book, one sees the import of the whole; the conclusion contains an appeal that emerges from a deeply patriotic feeling.

---

22. Jean-Jacques Rousseau, *The Social Contract*, trans. Charles M Sherover (New York: New American Library, 1974), 121 (translation altered).

23. Alberico Gentili, *De Legationibus*, III/9, cited in Maurizio Viroli, introduction to *The Prince* by Machiavelli, xix.

24. Machiavelli, *Prince*, chap. 26.

25. Ibid., chap. 15.

26. Ibid., chap. 17.

Machiavelli there expresses the misery of his fatherland, which had deteriorated into so many principalities and communities that constantly struggled against one another and thereby provided a playground for foreign invaders. Machiavelli declares the principle that everything else must give way to the unity of the state, as the highest law, and he suggests measures by which this could be achieved.[27]

While Machiavelli thus advises princes, he also, on the other side, advises citizens how to discern princes who have little reason to harm their subjects and are therefore to be loved; and how to avoid being deceived by princes who appear to be beneficent while concealing their cruelty. In view of the exhortation, those who understand would be prepared to join in the effort to free and unite Italy by following their leaders; they would, if capable, make use of Machiavelli's advice in order to discern those princes who would further this most worthy goal.

Machiavelli observes that there are cases in which there is complete concord between princes and citizens, that is, cases in which the prince will be well liked by the citizens. A number of cases of somewhat the same character are identified in the course of the account, and though, as in many cases, the identification takes the form of a description, typically there is advice at the core of the description. There is mention of cases in which—especially in new principalities—men decide to change their ruler, assuming that this will improve their lot, only then to see through their experience with the new ruler "that matters have become worse."[28] In this case the description entails the advice to citizens to be extremely wary of any change of rulers.

Machiavelli identifies certain cases in which the prince requires the assistance of the common people. One such case is that in which a prince sets out to invade and seize a region. Machiavelli writes: "Although someone may have the most powerful of armies, he always needs the support of the inhabitants to seize a region."[29] This imperative has two implications. First of all, it advises the prince that invasion alone does not suffice for seizing a region, for occupying it and assuming rule over it. But, secondly, the statement not only, on the positive side, advises the prince to employ the support of the inhabitants but also informs the inhabitants that they are necessary for the prince's exploits and that they can prevent occupation of their region by withdrawing—secretly perhaps—their support. Here again the two-sidedness, the double intention, of Machiavelli's discourse comes to light.

The Prince is a paradigm of engagement. As he surveys recent and current events, Machiavelli not only attests to them but also takes a stand for or against

---

27. Hegel, *Grundlinien der Philosophie des Rechts*, §255, *Zusatz*.
28. Machiavelli, *Prince*, chap. 3.
29. Ibid.

them. There is, for instance, his discourse on fortresses, which princes have been accustomed to erecting as secure shelters from sudden attack. He affirms the construction of such edifices: "I praise this method, because it has been employed since ancient times." On the other hand, his tone is one of condemnation when he mentions the demolition of two fortresses in Città di Castello and the razing of all the fortresses in Urbino. His engagement and its deepening become conspicuous as he lets the discourse drift toward metaphor: "the best fortress that exists is not to be hated by the people."[30]

In its engagements, its advisements, and its judgments, *The Prince* is not just a book but a political deed.

C. Invisible Polity

A few miles north of downtown Chicago, there is a small piece of land that juts out into Lake Michigan. In winter it is invaded by ice from the freezing water splashed up from the lake, and it completely covers the protective wall bordering the area. But now it is early summer, and the strong wind that blows constantly off the lake has lost its sting. It is a warm, clear day with excellent visibility, and the skyscrapers—the Hancock Building, the Sears Tower (now Willis Tower), and other tall buildings—are distinctly visible. But the one thing I cannot see is Chicago itself. I see the buildings. I see part of the long stretch of parkland between the buildings and the lake as it borders the built-up areas and visually implies the land on which all the buildings are erected. What I see, then, are buildings and land, but not the city itself. It is simply not visible. I decide to go in search of it, taking the train south to Michigan Avenue, where I see a great deal more of the city, pedestrians, streets, cars and passengers, buildings that are not tall enough to have been seen from my earlier outlook, and in these buildings shops, offices, and restaurants. But the city of Chicago is nowhere to be found. The city itself is invisible. It would be quite bizarre to suppose that, despite all the things seen, it does not exist. And yet, it is invisible, and there is not the least indication that somehow it will cease to be invisible, even though it is indisputably there. The decisive agency by which its presence is attested is not visual perception but rather imagination. Imagination gathers up the various visible moments, both those actually seen and those only implied by what is seen, and by taking up this manifold of visible moments, it brings to presence the city itself, posits it as actually there. But being-present, being-there, is not a matter of being visible to our sensible vision. Rather, the city shows itself as being there by being brought forth nonsensibly by imagination. The city itself remains invisible, and yet imagination attests to its being-there, to its actual presence.

---

30. Ibid., chap. 20.

So it is with all political abodes. They are invisible and yet are present.

One consequence is that, as invisible, a polity is unlike a thing and must, accordingly, be dealt with in a different manner. It is possible to determine that a thing, as it appears, is to be altered in a particular, thoroughly defined way and to carry out precisely that alteration. It is there before us in its visibility such that one can see exactly what one intends to alter about it and can proceed to do so. With a polity it is different because it is not visible. One may want to do something to it, to alter it (for example, to make it more just). But it is not there, and so one does not know what exactly is to be done to satisfy one's desire to alter it nor how to go about it. What is to be altered is indiscernible. Therefore, there will be multiple different opinions regarding the alteration, and often there will be conflict between them: one cannot discern a single, correct way to plan and carry out the alteration. If the conflict becomes especially intense, a resolution by political means will become necessary.

Polities are typically composed of multiple communities. Communities, in turn, typically belong to multiple polities; they are stretched across a nest of polities, though in any particular case there may be one polity that is dominant. Familial communities are brought together in a town, which lies in a state, which, in turn, is situated within a nation. One inhabits various polities in quite different ways, and certain modulations of one's character correspond to the pattern of one's involvement in these polities. Certain aspects of one's character as a citizen of a nation are determined by a system of beliefs and practices quite different from those accompanying one's belonging to a town.

The inclusion of communities in a polity can be represented as a transition. Hegel traces various ways in which this transition takes place:

> As the transition into a new principle, the expansion of the family develops in its worldly being in some cases though its peaceful expansion into a people [*zu einem Volke*], a nation, i.e., a group sharing a common natural origin; in other cases, it develops through the collection of scattered groups of families under the influence of an overlord's power or as the result of a freely willed union arising from intertwining needs and the reciprocity of their satisfaction.[31]

Although the relation between polities and communities is typically that in which a multiplicity of communities is assembled within a polity, there are also other ways in which they can be related. Three are especially conspicuous. First of all, there are communities that are more extensive than any polity, most notably, the terrestrial community and the mortal community. Yet, these communities are abstract in the sense that they are constituted by a single determination held in common: the community of all who have the earth in common and the community of all who share the bond to death. In concrete communities, on the other

---

31. Hegel, *Grundlinien der Philosophie des Rechts*, §181.

hand, multiple determinations are shared—as in a familial community where all are kin, all have a common language, certain beliefs are shared, and so forth. The second kind of relation is that in which the community is congruent with the corresponding polity, indeed, is identical with it. In this case the polity turns out to be a kind of community.[32] Gonzalo's commonwealth is a perfect—if extreme— example of this kind of relation; it is a polity in which everything is shared by all, that is, it is communal in the highest degree.

The third kind of relation between community and polity is the strongest and most extreme of all. In this case community is so contracted that it includes only two persons, who venture to break entirely with all other communities and with any polities to which these communities belong. A community of two lovers may withdraw in this fashion, forsaking even their familial communities and polity in their effort to preserve and strengthen their intimate commonality. In the case of mutually hostile families, the lovers may endeavor to forge a bond independent of the hostility between the families—sometimes recklessly, sometimes with disastrous consequences. They may seek such perfect community that it would border on its very annihilation as a community. Lovers may yearn to have all in common; even their sexuality may come to aim less at pleasure than at the most intimate communion and at the absolute exclusion of all that lies outside their union. Love would reach its utterly destructive extreme when, finally, all difference would be dissolved in the great nothing of death.

Shakespeare composed the play that has been handed down as the indisputable paradigm of such tragedy.

In the Prologue to *The Tragedy of Romeo and Juliet*, the chorus begins:

> Two households, both alike in dignity,
> In fair Verona, where we lay our scene,
> From ancient grudge break to new mutiny,
> Where civil blood makes civil hands unclean.
> From forth the fated loins of these two foes
> A pair of star-crossed lovers take their life.[33]

---

32. Near the beginning of the *Politics*, Aristotle traces the progression of stages of community: "So, the kind of community [κοινωνία] organized in accordance with nature [κατὰ φύσιν] for everyday life is a household [οἶκος]. . . . The first kind of community composed of more than one household, to serve purposes not of a daily sort, is a village [κώμη]. . . . The complete community made up of more than one village is a πόλις, since at that point, so to speak, it gets to the threshold of full self-sufficiency, coming into being for the sake of living, but being for the sake of living well" (1252b14–19, 28–31). This example illustrates the nesting structure: household within village within πόλις.

33. William Shakespeare, *The Tragedy of Romeo and Juliet*, in *The Riverside Shakespeare*, ed. G. Blakemore Evans (Boston: Houghton Mifflin, 1974), prologue, lines 1–6. Further references are to act, scene, and line.

The play follows the course thus laid out. As the lovers are thwarted in their intense desire for marriage, Romeo is forced to leave Verona for Mantua. Meanwhile Juliet is given a potion by which she will fall into a deep sleep resembling death, so as to avoid the unhappy marriage with Paris planned for the next day. When it is reported to Romeo that Juliet has died, he exclaims:

> Well, Juliet, I will lie with thee to-night.[34]

Buying poison, Romeo returns to Verona and at the feigned tomb of Juliet drinks the deadly, fast-working poison. When Juliet awakens and finds her lover dead, she stabs herself with his dagger. As the play ends, the Prince of Verona intones the final note of sorrow:

> For never was a story of more woe
> Than this of Juliet and her Romeo.[35]

* * *

Aristotle's pronouncement that "Man is by nature a political animal [ὁ ἄνθρωπος φύσει πολιτικὸν ζῷον]"[36] has often been echoed in the course of Western thought up through Hegel, who reformulated it in modern terms: "The rational determination of the human being is to live within a state, and if no state is there, then reason demands that one be founded."[37] And yet, man is also a natural being, an animal that, while being political by nature, also belongs to nature. Indeed, man can be determined by nature only if he has a bond to nature, only if to this extent he is a natural being. If Aristotle's pronouncement is granted, then it follows that the political abode as such cannot be thought without reference to the abode of nature.

Humans live in the midst of nature, and nature is the ultimate source of all the things necessary for the maintenance of human life. Destructive comportment to nature thus undermines the very conditions of life, as attested most powerfully by the destructive return of nature. For this reason, the submission of nature to purely human pursuits that are entirely oblivious to the ways of nature

---

34. Ibid., 5.1.34.
35. Ibid., 5.1.309–10.
36. Aristotle, *Politics* 1253a3.
37. This statement occurs in Hegel's 1822/23 lectures *Vorlesungen über Rechtsphilosophie* and is included in Alan White's translation of *The Philosophy of Right* (Newburyport, MA: Focus Publishing, 2002), §75. Another reformulation, a bit freer, was presented by Rousseau: "I had seen that everything is rooted in politics and that, whatever might be attempted, no people would ever be other than the nature of their government made them." Jean-Jacques Rousseau, *The Confessions* (New York: Penguin Books, 1953), 377.

is ultimately destructive. In place of assimilation and exploitation, what is called for is respect and forbearance for natural things.

Polities can be regarded as mediating between humans' political character and their bond to nature. On the one side, a polity is the locus of everything political, while, on the other side, a polity is bound to nature and draws from nature those resources that are vital to human life. It is because of the necessity of such mediation that Hegel insists that "if no state is there, then reason demands that one be founded." Because of the dependence of a polity on nature, the founding of a polity must always take into account proximity to a source of water and to land capable of providing food for the inhabitants of the polity. Climate must also be considered: it is unlikely that a polity will be built in the Arctic or in the middle of a vast desert. In the broadest terms, human comportment to nature will serve human well-being if exploitation is replaced by respect, by releasing nature to itself, and by recognizing and honoring the secret strength of things.

* * *

Beyond the cities built by humans as their most complex and extensive abode, there lies the expanse of the earth. Here nature largely prevails, and in the guise of its elemental forces it wreaks retribution for the violence to which humans submit it. Annihilation can advance from both directions, laying waste to the earth itself, rendering it uninhabitable.

Humans have never ceased dreaming of flight beyond the earth. There is no end to the dream, for even as superterrestrial flight is actualized, the vast panoply of the stars will continue to draw the dream ever farther. But, as the desolation of the earth continues without limit, the dream becomes one of desperation and of hope.

And yet, the transport of humans beyond the solar system to habitable planets around other stars will likely remain little more than a dream. Yet, recently certain projects have been proposed that would realize what up to now has remained merely a dream. The plan is to make use of certain technological innovations, which, though still today far from realizable, would render interstellar flight possible.[38] The plan calls for the use of huge ground-based lasers to accelerate large groups of tiny spacecrafts to enormous speeds. By being focused on these crafts' extremely thin, one-meter-wide sails, the protons produced by the lasers would impart such momentum to the spacecrafts that, so the theory— or perhaps the dream—goes, they would reach a velocity of approximately 20

---

38. The project is designated as the Starshot Breakthrough Initiative. It was proposed by Yuri Miner, Stephen Hawking, and Mark Zuckerberg.

percent of the velocity of light. A one-way trip to the nearest possible inhabitable exoplanet (Proxima b, which revolves around the star Proxima Centauri) would require twenty to thirty years.

Yet, some prominent scientists (such as Martin Rees) regard this project as too ambitious. In any case, even optimistic estimates predict that at least a quarter of a century will be needed for the necessary technology to be developed. And yet, even granted the possible success of this project, there remains an enormous difference between sending tiny spacecrafts to the stars and transporting humans across these vast distances. To say nothing of the capacity—or incapacity—of humans to endure decades of travel in space.

Thus, one cannot but suspect, almost to the point of certainty, that the prospect of transporting humans to habitable planets in other solar systems will remain, into the far distant future, little more than a dream. Until then, there will be no refuge for humans, no colonizing of the cosmos.[39] Should the earth be spoiled as a result of unbridled human errancy, there will be no recourse.

For a long time humans will be building their cities on the earth, and it is there that they will abide.

---

39. The possibility of human habitation *in* the solar system is minimal, almost nonexistent. The only possible candidates are Mars and Venus. Yet, the atmosphere of Mars consists of 95 percent carbon dioxide and less than 1 percent oxygen. There is very little water, which exists as vapor in the atmosphere. Its gravity is only about 38 percent of Earth's. Venus is extremely inhospitable. Its atmosphere consists mostly of carbon dioxide plus clouds of sulfuric acid. Its thick atmosphere traps the sun's heat, so that its temperature is more than 800° F.

6 Fecundity

A. Measured Growth

What renders something natural is its measured growth. Natural things do not grow at random; their growth is not deranged, disordered. Rather, their growth is subject to measure, which both restrains them and releases them onto their proper course. A child neither changes simply into an adult nor is transformed instantaneously, but grows into adulthood. As measured, growth is not necessarily an advance, not invariably a progression toward fulfillment: one can grow ill, one can grow old.

Animals, too, grow according to measure. A bear's retreat into hibernation will be responsive to the arrival of the cold, but a sense of measure, and not mere causality, will be involved in the choice of a suitable place. I have observed a squirrel that, as soon as snow began to accumulate, gave up his usual search for food and made a dash toward a thick shrub where there would be protection through the night. The growth of trees is also measured. In the forest the trees compete for the available sunlight needed for their photosynthesis, and each tree grows in a particular way so as to soak up some of the light.

As something that is rooted, a tree has the appearance of remaining entirely attached to its place, to the place where its seed sprouted and with proper measure it grew to maturity. In this respect it determines a place, which encompasses not just the tree itself but also its immediate surroundings, especially the ground in which it spreads out its roots. And yet, as Humboldt recognized, plants and, in particular, trees can shift away from their initial place. It can appear even that an entire forest moves; and indeed it can, though each tree contributes individually to the move by casting its seeds in a certain common direction. The growth of the trees, the way they grow, takes a different direction, as does, therefore, that of the forest as a whole. In most cases the shift reflects changing physical conditions; even if this transition does not appear to be entirely orderly and predictable, there is nonetheless a measure operative within it.

Measured growth can also occur in a secondary sense, supplementing the capacities of a natural being, in human beings of course, but also among higher animals: various skills may be developed, manual, intellectual, artistic. They will be gained in a measured way. One can learn an area in higher mathematics only by proceeding in a measured, not in a random, way; the ability to play a musical instrument can be developed only in a measured way; in a sense one grows into the ability.

It is highly unlikely that a cause underlying natural measure could be found; indeed it is questionable whether there could be any such cause, both because of the usual divergence between measure and cause and because unlike a cause, unlike any ἀρχή, measure is always bound closely to the natural form whose growth is measured by it. Is there an all-encompassing ἀρχή determining the development of ravens' capacity for such prelinguistic gestures as using their beaks to point to something[1] or for their pre-self-conscious recognition of themselves in a mirror?[2] Not likely, to say the least.

Nature is an abode that gives place to all natural things on the earth and that provides the setting within which character of all sorts (stabilization, self-reliance, etc.) can be shaped. Moreover, nature encompasses the anterior abodes and extends into them. This extension corresponds to the respective needs of those in the abodes and the concrete fulfillment of these needs. The region of nature surrounding a polity will be given over, in part, to agriculture and will be the main source of food for the citizens of the polity. The remaining woodlands will provide natural materials, which will serve various purposes in the polity, most notably, the production of artifacts. In turn, these products will be returned to those in the countryside, especially those things needed for agricultural purposes.[3]

The abode of nature encircles also that of being-alongside-another or being-together (with another): it is always in nature, even if secondarily, that one comes to be with another. Furthermore, it is as a natural being that one meets another, namely, as embodied. Even though one's proximal being exceeds one's body, it is nonetheless as a body that one directly appears. Among wild animals the ways of being together are, in most cases, quite different from those of humans. After I spread sunflower seeds on the ground, I observed squirrels and doves eating the seeds alongside one another as if—and this is what was remarkable—each were completely oblivious to those of the other species, those of one species quarreling over the seeds while totally ignoring the other species as though they were not present. Trees display their own kind of being-together, as when healthy trees

---

1. See Max Planck Institute, "'Look at That!' Ravens Use Gestures, Too," news release, November 29, 2011. Cited in Peter Wohlleben, *The Inner Life of Animals* (Vancouver/Berkeley: Graystone Books, 2017), 235.
2. See Jeremy Hance, "Birds Are More like 'Feathered Apes' than 'Bird Brains,'" *The Guardian*, November 5, 2016. Cited by Wohlleben, *Inner Life of Animals*, 109.
3. This description fits primarily certain regions in Europe and the United States and clearly would require modification in order to apply to some other regions. But it is the reciprocity between nature and polity that this example is meant to illustrate. It is important to observe also that the precise structures identified in this model undergo modifications in polities where relatively direct exchange is replaced by highly technological means of production.

pump sugar to distressed ones through their interconnected root system.[4] Even in the proximal abode of being-with-oneself as well as in its most intensive form, solitude, one is still engaged by nature, first as being of measured growth and then as drawing from nature many of the things needed for vital sustenance. The paradigm case, its reach exceeding all others, extending even beyond nature, is that of the one who seeks solitude by looking at the stars.

Nature often evokes wonder and occasions joy in the heart of those receptive to its allure. None express these sentiments more succinctly than Confucius: "The Master said: 'the wise find joy in waters; the benevolent [jen: 仁] find joy in mountains.'"[5] Emerson's testimony has a different texture and is more expansive. In a journal entry dated April 16–28, 1838, Emerson wrote: "Yesterday P.M. I went to the Cliff with Henry Thoreau. Warm, pleasant, misty weather which the great mountain amphitheatre seemed to drink in with gladness. A crow's voice filled all the miles of air with sound. A bird's voice, even a piping frog enlivens a solitude & makes world enough for us. At night I went out into the dark & saw a glimmering star & heard a frog & Nature seemed to say Well do not these suffice?"[6] The same might seem to be said by a stand of maple trees displaying their beautifully colored leaves in fall.

At the very outset of *Nature*, Emerson distinguishes between two senses of nature. On the one hand, there is nature in the common sense, which "refers to essences unchanged by man: space, the air, the river, the leaf."[7] Without marking

---

4. See E. C. Fraser, V. J. Lieffers, and S. M. Landhäusser, "Carbohydrate Transfer through Root Grafts to Support Shaded Trees," *Tree Physiology* 26 (2006): 1019–23. Cited by Peter Wohlleben, *The Hidden Life of Trees* (Vancouver/Berkeley: Greystone Books, 2016), 252.

It is perhaps too soon to determine the long-range effects that recent so-called radical botanical research will have. The goal of such research is to intensify by means of high technology the selective breeding and alteration of plants, which has been carried on for millennia and is responsible for transforming, for example, the tiny, foul-tasting kernels into what we call corn. Some of the research being conducted is designed to engineer plants that interact with humans; on the other hand, modifying tobacco plants so that their leaves glow in the dark (which is a prime example put forth) is not an impressive accomplishment. Whether such research will, as one advocate insists, "produce a far greener future, deepening humans' appreciation of flora in the process," and whether "tinkering with how plants work could be vital for their and our survival" will have to be tested by reference to what is essential and life-enhancing in the present—or at least less radical—modes of comportment to plants and to nature as such. See Linda Rodriguez McRobbie, "Plants Will Save Us—If We Help Them," *Boston Globe*, November 29, 2020, sec. K, 1, 4.

5. Confucius (Kongzi), *The Analects*, trans. D. C. Lau (Hong Kong: The Chinese University Press, 1979), bk. 6, no. 23. The passage can also be taken as referring to the Chinese conception of landscape and of landscape painting. According to this conception, the conjunction of waters (e.g., streams, waterfalls) and mountains (*shan-shui*) constitutes what in the West is termed landscape.

6. *Emerson in His Journals*, ed. Joel Porte, 185.

it, the enumeration broaches a distinction between natural things (the leaf) and natural elements (space, the air, the river). The degree to which each is immune to change varies accordingly: a leaf can be torn as it is ripped from a branch and can be crushed under foot; but space can in no wise be altered by human interaction.

On the other hand, there is nature in the philosophical sense. In this regard nature is "all that is separate from us, all which Philosophy distinguishes as the NOT ME"—that is, all things, "all other men and my own body"[8]—that is, in distinction from me, from the self, from the I. In determining the philosophical sense of nature in this manner, Emerson draws upon his profound, often unexpressed, appropriation of German Idealism. He takes over and rethinks the opposition between spirit and nature, an opposition that proves, at once, to be an identity: "behind nature, throughout nature, spirit is present."[9] In other words, spirit manifests itself in and through nature, so that, as Schelling expresses it, nature is visible spirit. For Emerson spirit does not directly manifest itself but comes to light in and through nature. In the mere song of a bird or the rhythmic croaking of a frog or in the sight of a star, spirit reveals itself to one with requisite sensibility. While retaining in general the prospect of spirit appearing in and through nature, Emerson focuses primarily on the concrete phenomena of nature, on the things belonging to nature in the common sense.

Yet, to maintain that nature manifests spirit does not entail that nature is— or can be transformed into—a transparent medium. No matter how revelatory it may be, nature guards its alterity; it refuses to pull its veil aside. If indeed the song of a bird can announce the presence of spirit in nature, the wildness of certain animals attests that nature holds much in secret.

Among the most enigmatic of the Fragments attributed to Heraclitus is the declaration that (roughly translated): "Nature loves to hide itself."[10] Nature's underlying measure, the measure of the growth of natural things, does not appear directly; neither can it simply be brought to appear as though convertible into a phenomenon. Rather, it grants only a trace, which can prompt a certain discernment, though without ever dispelling the surrounding obscurity. Yet, it is not only measure in a protracted—itself unmeasurable—sense that hides itself. There is also concealment of singularities, self-withholding of what has been called the secret strength of things. This is not merely the withdrawal operative in perceptual horizons but a hiddenness that is both prior to the unfolding of horizons and, almost paradoxically, on a surface reaching out beyond all horizonality. It is not just that in perception one cannot see the other side of the tree (the profile

---

7. Emerson, *Nature*, 4.

8. Ibid.

9. Ibid., 35.

10. φύσις κρύπτεσθαι φιλεῖ (Diels-Kranz B123). See my discussion in *The Figure of Nature*, chap. 3.

turned away from one's vision) but that in the bark—regardless of one's perspective—one senses that something lies hidden, the life of the tree to which the bark belongs but which itself retreats from every effort at apprehending it. In the bark one will never see the life of the tree, even though, in a perhaps unknown way, one recognizes that it is there. In the bark the life of the tree hides itself.

* * *

The most manifest display of one's belonging to nature is one's own body, which is the locus of the measured growth of humans. The body is the appearance of the self, the guise in which the self appears. Even in the intense look in the eyes of another, even in the sounding of the most sensitive voice, the self does not appear simply as itself but only as framed by the body. Yet, the self's outward comportment takes place not only as bodily appearance but also as signifying. In the classical formulations the body is the signifier of the soul. In signifying, preeminently in speech, the self reaches beyond itself in a manner that exceeds perception: the word *blue* outstrips any blue that can be seen, that is, one never sees blue as such.

It is by way of the body that the self's receptivity is made possible, its receptivity both of appearance and of significations. Already in antiquity vision was praised not only for the access it provides to mundane things but also as the source of the greatest benefit for us. As Timaeus said: "If we had not seen the stars or the sun or the heaven, no universal accounts—that is, no philosophy—would have been possible."[11] In fact, the eyes have a double capacity: not only their receptivity with respect to visible things but also, if regarded in connection with the face, their signifying capacity. The eyes of lovers can become so expressive that words become superfluous.

Audition is receptive in a manner different from that of vision, for sound is less localized than visibility and thus more comprehensive. But, most significantly, audition is the means for the reception of linguistic sound, of spoken words. Taken in total concentration, words constitute the λόγος and as such constitute, determine, the beginning of philosophy. In the voice of Heraclitus: "Listening not to me but to the λόγος. . . ."[12]

The primary complement to audition is the voice, the most subtle yet most powerful of all signifiers. Its dual character affords it an exceptional capacity: it can produce both pure tones and the articulated sounds of language. What is remarkable about song is that it blends tone and word into a seamless union.

Much less recognized as a signifier is the hand. The hand has the capacity to indicate, to point out, and thereby to refer to something, to draw attention to it. The hand functions as a kind of manual word and can to some extent be

11. Plato, *Timaeus* 47a.
12. οὐκ ἐμοῦ ἀλλὰ τοῦ λόγου ακουσαντας ... (Heraclitus, Fragment 50).

considered the precursor of language. In addition, the hands can be—and typically are—operative within speech, supplementing it with incipient sense, installing within it a spacing and a figuration, which are lacking in speech alone. Even in monologue, one may trace manually the shape of what one is saying to oneself.

Human receptivity is attuned to the many ways in which things can appear. There are those that show themselves by way of visible or audible appearance. There are those that appear only by letting the trail of their retreat remain perceptible. There are instances in which, without focusing on any particular thing, one senses an approaching danger or a perilous situation. There are still other appearances that are uplifting or captivating. Foremost among these is beauty. In contrast to merely appearing, there is a superlative mode of appearing, an appearing in which its very character as appearing is amplified. Such amplified appearing is beauty. In the constitution of beauty, mere appearing is transformed into shining. Yet, shining remains also an appearing set forth as apprehensible, and thus beauty is precisely shining-forth. That something is beautiful means that it shines forth in such a way as to be apprehensible in a sense that surpasses the mere apprehension of the qualities of things. Apprehension of beauty is exercised in an interplay with imagination such that there is, on the one hand, an apprehensive focus on the beautiful thing and, on the other hand, an imaginative drawing of the apprehension beyond the mere composite of qualities. Thus, beauty is a shining forth of the thing from itself.

A beautiful landscape—as such or as represented, for instance, in Cézanne's paintings of Mont Sainte-Victoire—does not just appear in the same manner as any mundane object. Rather, it shines forth to the observer in such a way as to enhance its colors, its contours, and the affinities between the things spread across the landscape. The beauty of the landscape lets all that belongs to it appear with intensified luminosity; in this light each shows itself as it itself is, as it truly is. In the event of beauty there is coincidence with truth and being.

It was once said that it is in and from nature that the gods appear. And yet, with their keen perceptiveness, the Greeks recognized that the gods never *simply* appear, never come to be directly present to human vision, but rather appear only as withdrawing from appearance, only as not appearing. Even in their temples there is only a simulation of their presence. Their appearance would always be privative: they would appear by leaving in nature traces of their withdrawing. But on occasions granted—so it was said—by Artemis, a glance might be offered in nature: an eagle soaring around the summit of a mountain, brilliant lightning in the night sky.

B. Elements of Nature

The proximity of nature to its elements, their unique concurrence, binds them together more inseparably than is the case with any other abodes. The elementals are not simply situated apart from nature: they are the elements *of nature*. There are elementals that, with only a certain change of perspective, can be regarded as belonging to nature. A vast forest stretching up the slopes of a mountain can be regarded as merely a collection of separate trees, and especially if one focuses on an individual tree, it has the appearance of a natural object, not of an elemental. On the other hand, there are elementals that are absolutely irreducible to a collection of natural things: the sky is not—and cannot be conceived as—a collection of skies.

In some cases the possibility of pluralizing functions as a determinant, the elemental then gathering and transforming what otherwise would be merely a multiplicity of natural things. Yet, there are elementals that are themselves plural: storms can occur in different locations and simultaneously without any incipient coherence.

The relation between the two abodes, that of nature or natural things and that of the elementals, is not exclusively one of encircling; it is not as though the elementals constituted only an outer boundary of nature, only an enclosing limit of natural things. To be sure, earth and sky do form such a boundary, delimiting the enchorial space within which, especially at the base of which, all events of nature take place. But other elementals traverse this space of nature or even occur entirely within it. It is as though lightning were hurled from on high down to the earth, threatening all things that lay in the area where it would strike. A winter storm covers the ground with deep snow, burying the food on which natural creatures such as birds depend. The oak forest spreads acorns across the ground, providing nourishment for such animals as squirrels. The wind gives voice to the verdant summer leaves. The elementals are the primary sources of the forces of nature, some bounteous and plentiful, some threatening and destructive.

All elementals have as a common feature a degree of indefiniteness; they are not determinately bounded in the manner in which things are. As they spread into their expanse, their borders remain vague. It is indefinite just where the rain shower begins and ends; its boundary varies constantly, and the direction in which it shifts is determined to an extent by other factors such as wind. It can also be quite difficult to decide definitively just where the limits of a mountain range lie. Along the line following the descent from the higher peaks to the progressively lower mountains and on downward toward the valley, it is rarely possible to mark a point where the range stops. The wind is even more elusive: while one may realize that the chilling wind one feels comes from the north, its exact whence and whither remain indefinite.

There are elementals that, as the most expansive, are absolutely encompassing, namely, earth and sky. They completely encompass enchorial space, bounding it as the place where nearly everything that concerns living beings happens. They encompass the entire abode of nature and constitute its receptacle as its outer, bounding limits. There are also other elementals that are encompassing though in ways different from that of earth and sky. A thunderstorm in a mountain valley can encompass an entire stretch of the valley, the low cloud cover enclosing it from above, the lower slopes of the mountains bounding its sides, the indefinite extension of the storm itself marking its expanse within the valley. A flash of lightning may momentarily illuminate the otherwise enshrouded valley, encompassing it with an incomparable brilliance. At such elemental sites as that of a storm, several elementals can intersect, overlap, or envelop one another: not only the lightning but also the accompanying thunder that echoes up the valley, the heavy rain that drenches everything not protected from it, and the wind sweeping down the valley form a concurrence of elementals. Indeed, a storm is precisely such a concurrence.

All living things are exposed to such elements. Whether threatened by a violent storm or caught unexpectedly in a gentle rain, one will seek shelter, even though few shelters are entirely secure: a storm can reduce a house to rubble, a roof may collapse under the weight of accumulated snow, or a stroke of lightning may set fire to one's shelter. Such natural, elemental disasters are decisively beyond human control, and the only recourse for humans is to retreat into a relatively safe place. Yet, at the pole opposite that of such threats, there is incomparable beauty in nature: nothing shines forth more brilliantly than the blue sky of a summer day patterned with various configurations of clouds. Or the falling snow as it slowly and silently covers the field as far as one can see. Or the swirling leaves and slowly swaying branches wrought by the gentle autumn breeze. Or the rainbow, product of sun and rain.

Most elementals are gigantic in the sense that they indefinitely exceed in magnitude all the things with which humans commonly deal as well as humans themselves and indeed all living things. It is not just a matter of being larger than all things including those of nature; rather, their magnitude is so great that no measure is possible by which to compare them to things. There is no proportionality that would link them to things, no comparison between them and the average height, for instance, of a human being. The expanse of the sky is paradigmatic: there are no evident indications as to what it would even mean to compare the height of a human being to the height or the expanse of the sky. Towering mountains are similarly gigantic, even if not in quite such an absolute manner as the sky. In the case of the mountains and of other elementals as well, the gigantic magnitude may take on also the form of sublimity. Such enhancement is found in those cases in which the excessive magnitude of the gigantic element has the effect of drawing the imagination upward in such a way as to evoke both an awareness of the essentially unlimited reach of the imagination and a sense of the sublimity—the elevation—of the one imaginatively engaging the sublime element. Gigantic—sublime—nature evokes an imaginative ascendancy that simulates reaching the upper limit of the gigantic so as to disclose, from that point, the imaginative capacity (δύναμις) that has enabled the ascent.

The fact that many elementals are gigantic is one reason, among others, that they cannot become private property and cannot be used up, consumed. Hegel designates certain things as universal or elemental: "The sea, etc., are elemental things." Then, referring to such things, he writes: "I cannot take universal things into possession; they are mine only as long as I have them. Thus it is when I breathe in air. . . . Particular things are consumed by being used, but universal things, like the sea, the air, etc., are not consumed."[13] On the other hand, when Hegel turns to consideration of nature and natural things, the contrast could not be starker. He describes nature as "sleeping spirit"[14]; and in more explicit terms, he writes that "everything spiritual is better than any product of nature."[15] Still further he advocates "the absolute human right to the appropriation [*Zuneigungsrecht*] of all things." The animal he considers "a thing," and he regards it as a mark of higher culture to realize "that among external things, there is nothing that is simply to be respected"—that everything is "only material" for human freedom, for the human will.[16] The consequence is striking: as a result of Hegel's negativity as regards nature along with his concept of universal things, he in effect draws precisely the distinction between nature and the elemental. On the other hand, his uncompromising subordination of nature to spirit and the human will broaches an absolute subjectivism, despite the fact that in other contexts—as early as *Faith and Knowledge*[17]—he distances himself from such one-sidedness.

While universal things or elementals cannot as such be possessed, their form as elemental can be reduced, even to the point where this form is entirely dissipated. This process is perhaps most conspicuous in the case in which it is reduced to land. This reduction is foreshadowed by the establishment of agriculture, which, however, is not yet a reduction of the earth but a working of the soil that releases the bounty of the earth. Marx describes, as an initial phase, an arrangement that involves only a slight progression beyond the simple agricultural condition: specifically, he describes the initial form assumed by land at the stage of feudal landed property. At this stage a certain bond to the land remains, and

---

13. The first of the two statements occurs in a *Zusatz* in Hegel's 1818/19 lectures *Die Philosophie des Rechts* and, also in a *Zusatz*, in his 1824/25 lecture *Vorlesungen über Rechtsphilosophie*. The second statement occurs in a *Zusatz* in Hegel's 1817/18 lectures *Die Philosophie des Rechts* They are included in Alan White's translation of *Philosophy of Right*, §46.
14. Hegel, *Grundlinien der Philosophie des Rechts*, §258.
15. Hegel, *Ästhetik* (Westberlin: Verlag das europäische Buch, 1985), 1:40. First appeared, edited by H. S. Hotho, in 1835.
16. Hegel, *Grundlinien der Philosophie des Rechts*, §44.
17. Hegel, *Glauben und Wissen* (Hamburg: Felix Meiner, 1962), 18f. First published in 1802/03.

in this respect there is not yet a severing of all connection with the earth; both the lord and the serfs who work the land regard themselves as belonging to the land. Yet, according to Marx's analysis, this bond is eventually broken, and as the earth is entirely reduced, as it is denatured, the land is "dragged completely into the movement of private property"[18]—that is, the relation of humans to the earth becomes one of possession, violating the integrity of the earth as such. The land becomes a commodity, a matter of capital: land "sinks to the status of a commercial value."[19] The earth as such in its originary form will have been lost sight of.

Another denaturing of an elemental is under way in the commercial venture—mentioned in chapter 3—to launch a huge number of satellites, which will drastically alter the appearance of the night sky. Not only will the age-old practice of observing the stars and the constellations be disrupted by the satellites' reflection of sunlight back to the earth, but also certain areas of basic astronomical research will suffer serious interference. In effect, the satellites will produce a denaturing of the sky. No less than the capitalist reduction of the earth, the launching of these fake stars will reduce the very appearance of the night sky to a matter of commercial value. For even if seemingly beneficial goals such as universal provision of internet are put forth for public consumption, the venture is entirely motivated by the commercial benefits that certain corporations will obtain. Far from serving the good of all people, the venture will serve only to increase the profit of a few.

To denature both the earth and the sky is to disrupt the very space within which humans—and indeed all living things—have their natural abode. It is to contaminate with narrow commercial values all that is delimited by earth and sky. It is to commit a kind of elemental thievery.

*   *   *

The comportment of humans to the elementals is determined to a significant extent by the various modes of motion belonging to the respective elements of the elemental abode. The motion exemplified by the earth is the privative mode: the earth is immovable. If, specifically, the earth is regarded not as a body in space but as belonging to an abode of humanity—and indeed of all living things—then the only forms of motion that can be attributed to it are such limited phenomena as earthquakes, avalanches, and volcanic eruptions. At least, these are the phenomena within the range of human memory; from geological research it is

---

18. Karl Marx, *Economic and Philosophic Manuscripts of 1844*, trans. Martin Milligan (Amherst, NY: Prometheus Books, 1988), 64.
19. Ibid.

known that in the remote past such cataclysmic events as the shifting of entire continents occurred.

The immobility of the earth is described by Husserl in his late manuscript "Grundlegende Untersuchungen zum Phänomenologischen Ursprung der Räumlichkeit der Natur."[20] He writes: "The *Ur-Arche* earth does not move." The word *Arche* denotes, on the one hand, *ark*, as in Noah's ark: all living things are loaded onto—that is, supported by—the ark, the earth. On the other hand, taken as ἀρχή, the word means *origin*, the basis on which all things rest. He also refers to the earth as the *Urheimat*, that is, as humanity's primal home, as the all-supporting stability provided by the earth. Yet, though the earth does not move, this does not entail that it is at rest. In Husserl's words: "In its originary form of representation, the earth itself does not move and is not at rest; rest and motion have sense only in relation to it." Finally, Husserl makes the transition from earth to sky: "If earth is constituted [in this way], then sky too is necessary as the field of what is outermost yet still spatially experienceable for me and for all of us—from the earth-basis."

One can say of the sky what Husserl said of the earth: that it neither moves nor is at rest. Moreover, both the diurnal and the nocturnal sky are largely uniform, except at the time of the transition from one to the other, at dawn and dusk. The depth of the sky is unlike that of any other elemental: it displays no depth whatsoever, not even when there is movement in it, the regular movement of the sun and the moon in their orbits, the drifting of sunlit cumulus clouds across the sky. For humans, relishing always the upward way, the sky represents absolute height and never ceases to draw human vision, hope, and aspirations upward.

There are lakes that can be so still that often they are like mirrors reflecting, sometimes almost perfectly, the woods around the edge of the water. But most bodies of water—whether on the scale of an elemental or not—display motion either on their surface or in the direction they are flowing: streams and rivers, bays and oceans, the cove on the coast of Maine opening onto the ocean, the gentle waves lapping onto shore. From the fear of a violent storm at sea threatening the lives of those aboard a ship to the meditative receptiveness to the sound of a tiny brook or of the gentlest of waves, human comportment to the motion or stillness of water assumes innumerable forms so various as to resist any classification. Impressions of the sea, even if imaginary, can be so strong that even in a painting of the sea—for instance, a work by Turner depicting a storm at sea—it may be as if, when absorbed in the scene, one can hear the raging tempest as one gazes on the threatened ships.

20. Edmund Husserl, "Grundlegende Untersuchungen zum Phänomenologischen Ursprung der Räumlichkeit der Natur," in *Philosophical Essays in Memory of Edmund Husserl*, ed. Marvin Farber (Cambridge, MA: Harvard University Press, 1940), 307–26. See my extensive analysis of this text in *Double Truth* (Albany: State University of New York Press, 1995), 43–55.

Other elementals evoke various kinds of comportment. Air, itself invisible, can only be felt and then only in the form of wind, which, depending on the surroundings, may or may not be audible. Lightning, appearing as pure light in motion, can call forth various responses ranging from fear to fascination. It may appear in the distance, lighting up the horizon, so remote that it creates no particular concern; one is merely a spectator with no further involvement. But when lightning is flashing brilliantly as it concurs with other elements to form a severe storm, everything is different. In a journal entry from September 6, 1854, Thoreau portrays such a scene. Yet, he casts his description from such a great distance that no other element involved in the storm can be perceived; it is as though everything surrounding the lightning had been blocked out, bracketed, so that what presents itself for the description is the pure lightning. Thoreau's words:

> There is now approaching from the west one of the heaviest thunder-showers (apparently) and with the most incessant flashes that I remember to have seen. It must be twenty miles off, at least, for I can hardly hear the thunder at all. The almost incessant flashes reveal the form of the cloud, at least the upper and lower edge of it, but it stretches north and south along the horizon further than we see. Every minute I see the crackled lightning, intensely bright, dart to earth or forkedly along the cloud. It does not always dart *direct* to earth, but sometimes very crookedly, like the bough of a tree, or along the cloud forkedly. . . . And each time, apparently, it strikes the earth or something on it with terrific violence.[21]

In another journal entry entitled "History of the Sky," Thoreau describes a cloud advancing in a way similar to that of the lightning:

> Sometimes, when I go forth at 2 P.M., there is scarcely a cloud in the sky, but soon one will appear in the west and steadily advance and expand itself, and so change the whole character of the afternoon and of my thoughts. The history of the sky for that afternoon will be but the development of that cloud.[22]

The title of this entry is provocative. For the sky has no history, cannot have a history, since it does not move. Except for the perfectly regular alternation between day and night, the sky is uniform. There can be movement only by those things that, like clouds, move against the uniform background of the sky, those things that give texture to the uranic elemental.

Thunder is the audible companion of lightning, though its form of movement is unique. Contrary to common parlance, thunder does not roll, though

---

21. Carl Bode, ed., *Selected Journals of Henry David Thoreau* (New York: New American Library, 1967), 204.
22. Henry David Thoreau, Journal entry of February 18, 1860, in *The Journal of Henry D. Thoreau*, ed. B. Torrey and F. H. Allen (Boston: Houghton Mifflin, 1906), 13:154.

it does indeed advance. It is sound moving, sound that is not the sound of anything. Just as in the flashing of lightning there is nothing that flashes but only the flashing, so it is with thunder: there is not something that thunders but just the sounding. Even granting the role of air in the production of thunder, it is nonetheless not as though the air thunders, not as though air were the subject of the thundering. There can be sharp thunder as well as thunder that, by its echoes, is repetitive. There is distant thunder, which is more uniform and seems quite stationary—almost as if the earth itself were sounding.

In elemental nature, specifically in thunder and lightning, there is a repetition of the beginning; that is, reflection on these phenomena returns this discourse, momentarily, to the beginning. As sound moving, thunder reveals a space and does so audibly. Lightning, in turn, is pure moving light; it is light casting its gift. Thus, in the dyad of thunder and lightning, there is a phenomenal repetition of the beginning, of the originary dyad of space and luminosity.

In their way of presenting themselves, there is a fundamental difference between elementals and things. Without exception things present themselves by way of profiles. A thing is always seen from some perspective, and to this perspective the thing presents itself by means of a particular, limited profile. One never sees the thing as a whole. One can vary the perspective, looking at the thing from a different angle, but with each new profile that is seen, the profiles seen from previous perspectives are no longer seen. To gain a new perspective is to lose what one saw from the previous perspective, and thus there is no accumulation of profiles that eventually would reveal the thing in its entirety. No matter how directly one focuses one's vision on the thing, it always faces also in other directions. The same perspectival character belongs also to other forms of apprehension, though there is less distinct articulation due to the weaker directionality of the other senses.

Elementals, on the other hand, do not present themselves by way of profiles. It makes no sense to suppose that one can assume various perspectives, for example, on the sky, which in its utter uniformity can present no profiles. The sky is the same from everywhere; not even the clouds floating across it present profiles. The storm that enshrouds the mountain valley shows no profiles; it encompasses the valley rather than remaining withdrawn into unseen profiles. A streak of lightning across the nocturnal sky could hardly be less geared to perspectival presentation; to say nothing of thunder as it advances down the valley and echoes from other nearby mountains,

The elementals engage one's vision in a different way. Rather than prompting a vision that would circulate through several perspectives, seeking to observe a number of profiles sufficient to reveal the thing (though not in its entirety), the elementals draw one's vision forth, entice one to look beyond, to gaze farther into the distance. At first, one looks merely across the valley but soon is impelled to gaze still farther toward the higher mountains beyond rather than lingering in the foreground. If the distant mountains appear to be enshrouded in mist, this hints that they may be more distant than one would have supposed, and in this case their attractive force may be all the greater.[23] It is likewise with the sea. One's vision can hardly remain focused merely on the gentle waves that wash up on the shore; rather, one will be enticed to look out across the sea into the distance, which becomes progressively more unmeasurable, which goes on and draws one's vision even beyond what one can actually see, extending the distance by way of imagination.

On a much smaller scale, picture a cove on a rocky coast from the landward side of which one can see, at the far edge of the cove, an island and an opening onto the ocean—or rather, which one *could* see, were the cove and everything beyond it not enshrouded in fog. Suppose then that the fog begins to dissipate, first on the landward side, the point of observation, and gradually recedes across the cove until eventually one can see the island and the opening onto the ocean. This receding is precisely an enactment, in nature, of the drawing of vision into the distance.

There is also a cosmic enactment, a spanning of the greatest distance of all, almost unimaginable in its remoteness from all other human abodes. One's vision can be drawn forth in such a way that its counterpart is to enter into solitude.

Among the elementals there are concurrences of various kinds. The one that gathers the most elements is a thunderstorm. In such a concurrence wind, rain, lightning, thunder, and often a mountainous landscape come together, blending their motions, also in the instances of wind, rain, and thunder, blending their voices. Some are thoroughly mixed, namely, rain and the wind that can drive it, as well as lightning and the thunder that usually accompanies it.

There are simpler concurrences that, in a sense, are determined by certain natural things. Plants, in particular, have such a conjunctive capacity, which derives from the fact that they are both aerial and terrestrial. Coccia expresses and elaborates this fact: "It is as though a plant lived two lives at the same time: one aerial, bathed and immersed in light, made of visibility and of an intense interspecific interaction with other plants and with other animals of all kinds; the other chthonic, mineral, latent, *ontological*, nocturnal, chiseled in the stony flesh of the plant."[24] Plants belong, then, to two different spaces; the leaf is the paradigmatic form, born and sustained from the roots of the tree, yet producing oxygen and freeing it into airy space. Thus, the plant exemplifies and gives space to a concurrence of earth and sky, of terrestrial and aerial.

---

23. This is a technique commonly used in classical Chinese landscape painting: as the distance from the main mountain increases, this increasing distance is represented by increasing enshroudment in the form of mist and clouds.

Interaction between elementals and natural things occurs not only in the case of plants in general but also in numerous other ways. Consider, for example, the delicate leaves spread out on the branches of a small birch tree as they sway gently in the breeze, in the elemental, invisible movement of the air. Or think of the swaying of the branches on a pine tree and the changing configurations of the needles. In these simple occurrences, individualized nature and the elemental air come together and show that, in their difference, they nonetheless belong together.

Another way in which natural things and elementals come together and display how they belong together occurs as the growth of particular kinds of things from the earth. Many trees have roots that are exposed above ground, and in this way show, indeed most manifestly, how they are rooted in the earth. Moreover, trees require rain and sunlight if they are to prosper. Still further, bordering on the symbolic, their verticality gestures toward the sky, doubling, as it were, their search for maximum sunlight as they spread out their crown.

Fire, too, as elemental, often interacts with natural things such as trees, and not only destructively. John Muir told of witnessing a roaring fire as it approached a grove of sequoias. Most remarkably, when the fire reached these giant conifers, it "became calm, like a torrent entering a lake"; it merely crept along the ground, "slowly nibbling the cake of compressed needles."[25] Muir described the sequoias' amazing ability to withstand such fires whenever, after a few years, there were shrubs and undergrowth around the trees, which in fact needed the fire in order to clear bare soil for their seeds. Muir remained somewhat skeptical regarding the benefit of such fires, though comparison with later examples of fires in logged-out forests confirmed the supposition regarding the purpose served by the capacity of the sequoias to withstand and indeed benefit from such fires.

By thinking the togetherness of elementals and natural things at a fundamental level, the way is prepared for an exorbitant conception of nature. This conception would be set outside previous metaphysical conceptions in that nature would no longer be thought by reference to an ἀρχή. It would be referred neither to an archaic nature beyond nature nor to an archaic interiority or subjectivity. Rather, nature would now be thought without reference to any ἀρχή whatsoever. In place of a grounding of things in an ἀρχή, the operative determination would consist of a particular way in which elementals and natural things come together, as, for instance, earth and sky, themselves brought together, come together with a leaf. From a privative point of view, such a conception will appear anarchic; but,

---

24. Emanuele Coccia, *The Life of Plants: A Metaphysics of Mixture* (Cambridge: Polity Press, 2018), 82. Coccia cites the extremely succinct statement by Charles Bonnet: "Plants are planted in the air nearly as much as they are in the earth" (44).

25. Cited by Zach St. George, *The Journeys of Trees* (New York: W. W. Norton, 2020), 24–25.

regarded affirmatively, it is a conception that frees the things of nature for their emplacement amidst the elements of nature.

* * *

At the Fram Museum in Oslo, there are exhibitions of sailing vessels used in various expeditions to reach the North or South Pole. Attention to the exhibitions lets one understand that on such expeditions there is an intensification of the relation that humans sustain to the elemental. Specifically, there is a response to the resistance offered by the elemental, a longing to engage with the elemental and to sustain oneself in and through it. There is no question of mastery, for whereas one can master things, one will never master the elemental, for example, the expanse of ice near the poles. Such engagement requires courage in a sense that must be redetermined in relation to the elementals.

Perhaps, in general, courage always has to do with engaging something elemental, as in braving a storm or venturing forth on an uncharted expanse of ice. This is also, to some degree, a matter of engaging the proper elementals, those elements that belong to the very essence of the self, a matter of risking death while also drawing on the depth of self, which is neither transparent nor controllable. One engages these elementals of the self as, at the same time, one engages the elementals of nature.

This is a way of understanding courage *outside* the political sphere. Perhaps courage as exercised in the πόλις and its descendants should be redetermined *from* this elemental awareness. And perhaps this is indeed courage in the most originary sense.

7 Cosmic Visions

A. Sunlight

An ancient poet, one said to have been blind, wrote repeatedly that to live is to behold the light of the sun. It is as though the truth of these words shone so brilliantly that they were visible even to one bereft of vision.

When, on a clear, bright day, one looks upward through the lofty expanse of air, upward toward the heavens, it is the sun that is the most prominent sight. On such a day, it appears as the source of the luminosity that makes visibility possible, that lets all things be seen, while itself withdrawing almost into invisibility. When there is cloud cover, its withdrawal is, though paired with a different kind of luminosity, no less manifest.

It also allows things of nature to undergo the measured growth that belongs intrinsically to them, that defines them as natural. To an extent, quite immeasurable, it determines the measure of their growth.

It is also the primary natural clock. The rising and setting of the sun and its daily course across the heavens make time visible, translate time into space. It has indeed been said that the sun determines the most natural measure of time, the day. Its presence is day, the gift of sunlight; its absence is night, the veil of darkness. Animals come and go by day or by night, as is their way. In their polities, humans retreat with the coming of night, in accord with their ἦθος.

It defines the seasons, as it makes its way between winter solstice and summer solstice. Living things follow its course, from the austerity of winter to the rebirth that arrives with spring, from the bounty of summer to the colors of autumn.

In its rising and setting, it displays colors that are among the most brilliant to be seen: the orange glow of a cloudless sunset, the streaks of color interspersed with the clear sky, the promise of light as the night gives way to the day. Attesting to the brilliance of these colors, the blind poet writes of the rosy fingers of the young dawn.

And yet, the sun itself resists being directly seen, allowing only a glance before repelling our vision. The ancients tell of the danger that vision incurs when, during an eclipse, one can look directly at the sun—at least at the corona—without being repelled. Blindness can result, even though one will not—and then never will—have actually seen the sun. The very source of all visibility guards its own invisibility, verges on invisibility.

The sky invites free, open, unhindered vision. The clearer the day, the more likely it is that one's vision will be absorbed by the unspeakable beauty of the blue that shines forth from the sky. Yet, even the clouds that may block this view, in whole or in part, often convey their protension (dark, threatening, drifting, etc.) and configuration (cirrus, nebulous, etc.). And yet, night teaches that without sunlight the blue dissolves, melts away into darkness. It is then that one may have a sense of gazing directly into the cosmos. On a clear night the stars enhance this sense and convey an awareness of aloofness and remoteness; though always present, they are inaccessible. The stars have a remarkable capacity to activate the imagination and to engender visions of fantastical figures in the sky. They also have the power of evoking moods and affections that are otherwise rarely experienced; much the same power belongs to the magic of moonlight.

Sun, sky, stars, moon—these are the things one may see when one's vision is cast skyward. Barring cloud cover, these things show themselves to unaugmented vision; at the appointed time they will always be visible. By day or night, as is proper to each, their aura forms the upper limit of the enchorial space in which things come to pass and in which humans, in particular, abide. The expanse of the heavens is like a dome over all things; it is a protocosmic abode, which shows itself to unaided vision.

And yet, from the moment when Galileo, peering through the newly invented telescope, discovered that there are mountains on the moon (that it does not have a smooth, perfect surface), that there are more than ten times the number of fixed stars than were previously visible (that they are at different distances from the earth, not fixed to an outer Ptolemaic sphere), and that Jupiter has four moons (that not all bodies revolve around the earth, which thus proves not to be the center of the universe), everything is different. An astronomical vision, surpassing ordinary, unaided vision, comes into play; it effects both an enhancement of the visibility of the phenomena accessible to ordinary vision and an extension of vision beyond the limits operative in such vision. The difference is decisive: while the view corresponding to ordinary vision is largely unchanging or at least regularly cyclical, astronomical vision continually progresses, exploring ever more closely the less remote phenomena and extending its investigations ever farther to the more distant reaches of the cosmos.

Astronomical vision is not always direct; it does not necessarily yield an actual view of the phenomenon being investigated. For example, one of the principal ways in which the search for exoplanets is carried out is based on measurement of the minuscule decrease in the luminosity of the star around which the planet revolves as it passes in front of the star. The planet itself cannot be seen even with the currently most powerful telescopes; its presence, its existence, can only be inferred on the basis of its measurably visible effect. Its own visibility is withheld even from the sharp eye of the telescope.

Another example illustrates even more clearly the limit of astronomical vision. Though the velocity of light is absolutely maximal, an enormously long period of time is required for it to traverse the space between a distant star and the earth. Thus, the view that this light conveys (normally just a point of light) is that of the star as it was at the time when the light was emitted. In other words, one sees the star as it was in a very remote past, not as it *is*—if it still *is*—at the time when it is observed on earth. The view of the star belongs to a remote time, which is equal to the length of time required for the light to travel from the star to the earth. The star is not only spatially distant but also temporally distant; indeed its spatiality renders it temporally distant. Its presence belongs to the past.

Starlight cannot even be termed, in the proper sense, *phenomenon*, since a hiatus between presence and past belongs to its very mode of self-showing. And yet, despite the strangeness of the luminous distances it involves, the cosmos has the character of an abode for humans. It is the ultimate abode, the abode that encompasses all other abodes, the ἦθος to which all other ἤθη are subordinate.

* * *

We, all of us, lead a double life. While our vision is directed at one and the same sight, the spectacle that we actually have in view is seen as double; it is seen as if it were—almost at least—two different spectacles. We see sun, sky, stars, moon. They are seen immediately, as soon as we cast our vision upward. We see them as forming or belonging to the dome that, bordered on the lower side by the earth, encloses the enchorial space in which all things come to pass. And yet, while continuing to see this spectacle, which to a large extent provides the directives needed for everyday life, we also—with astronomical vision leavened by imagination—look beyond into the cosmos. All that we saw previously in everyday vision now appears otherwise. The sky melts away into the blackness of space (anticipated by the darkness of night); the sun is a generator of light and heat driven by the fusion of elements; the stars are distant suns; and the moon is merely a barren, rocky sphere circling the earth. With the inception of astronomical vision, we see both spectacles. They are the same and yet not the same—a kind of celestial identity and difference.

B. Beyond the Sky

Modern astrophysics has shown that there are billions of galaxies, each containing billions of stars. In addition, it has discovered many phenomena that previously would have been inconceivable, phenomena such as dark matter, neutron stars, and black holes. And yet, the cosmos consists almost entirely of space, of empty or near-empty space.

In turning to the question of space at the level of the cosmos, the present discourse circles around to the beginning, or, equivalently, returns to the beginning. For it is from the genesis beginning with luminous space that the discourse has made its way to the all-inclusive, ultimate abode. In their very identity, there is no greater difference than that between the void of luminous space and the comprehensiveness of the cosmic abode.

Space is invisible. One sees things in nature, nearby objects and distant mountains, but one does not see the space in which these things are situated. On a bright, sunny day, one gazes upward at the azure sky and steals a quick glance at the sun; but one does not see the space between earth and sky, nor that in which the brilliant rays of sunlight can be glimpsed. One cannot but sense that space is there, and it is possible to find surrogates—rising fog, for instance—capable of offering a certain intimation of space. One will say that space is there where things are manifest. Yet, it is not as though there is first of all a *there*, which then comes to be occupied by space. The *there* is none other than space.

While one cannot see space as such, one can see the things that fill space and to that extent can acquire a certain vision of space. In Hegel's words: "One cannot point out any space that would be space itself; rather it is always filled space and never separated from what fills it."[1] Such a vision of "filled space" comes about most conspicuously when what fills the space shares its form and detaches itself from the space.

The reference to the vision of filled space assumes a much stronger form in the thesis that empty space does not exist at all. In the course of the mathematical elaboration of the theory of gravitation provided by the general theory of relativity, Einstein asserts: "On the basis of the general theory of relativity . . . space as opposed to 'what fills space' . . . has no separate existence." He adds: "There is no such thing as an empty space, i.e., a space without field. Space-time does not claim existence on its own, but only as a structured quality of one field."[2]

Experimental confirmation of this thesis—or at least strong evidence for it—has been provided by the discovery of cosmic microwave background radiation.

---

1. Hegel, *Enzyklopädie der philosophischen Wissenschaften im Grundrisse. Zweiter Teil: Die Naturphilosophie* (Frankfurt a.M.: Suhrkamp, 1970), §254, *Zusatz*.
2. Albert Einstein, *Relativity: The Special and the General Theory* (New York: Crown Publications, 1961), 155.

This phenomenon has a fixed wavelength, a distinctive spectrum, and a temperature three degrees above absolute zero. Most remarkably it is almost perfectly isotropic and is entirely pervasive throughout the observable universe. Thus, even if seemingly empty, even if entirely devoid of things and even of the cosmic dust that is common in outer space, space is thoroughly permeated by this evenly distributed radiation.

In fact, however, recent discoveries have shown that cosmic microwave background radiation is not perfectly isotropic, for there exists a "cold spot," which is a fraction of one degree colder than the rest. Though questions remain and research continues, the evidence indicates that the cold spot is caused by the influence of a supervoid. Supervoids are vast areas between the filaments along which galaxies are lined up. These voids are among the largest structures in the universe, stretching nearly two billion light-years across. Since they have a much lower density of galaxies than other areas of space, they have weaker gravitational forces. As a result the particles of the cosmic microwave background radiation, which normally rely on gravity, require more energy to travel across a supervoid and hence lose energy. Recent research indicates that it is this loss of energy that causes the cold spot.

In view of the anomaly of the cold spot, it appears that even what otherwise would be the most uniform, the most evenly distributed energy in the universe, admits an area of nonuniformity. Yet, this anomaly does not undermine the conclusion that there is no empty space, that all space is filled, even though quite thinly and slightly less than uniformly.

C. The Retreat of Visibility

More than any other discourse, that concerning the cosmic abode calls for a certain engagement with the results of recent scientific research. In this connection such discourse would begin to bridge the gap between philosophical discourse and scientific developments, a gap that has been all too prominent throughout much of the post-Newtonian era. The remarkable advances on both sides—even if in different senses—make it highly appropriate that neither remain isolated from the other.

From the side of philosophy, the gap is a result largely of efforts to relativize, reduce, or undermine a large range of scientific discoveries on the ground that they are conditioned by a prior projection. The supposition is that a conceptual structure already in place is presupposed by such discoveries and thus renders them secondary and dependent on these concepts. And yet, such a supposition is difficult to sustain in light of such direct discoveries as Galileo's discovery of the moons of Jupiter; for, regardless of the conceptual expressions used, *there are* moons around Jupiter. Even for theoretical-experimental connections that are much more complex, there seems to be little possibility of appealing to a presupposed conceptual structure that would be capable of undermining the connection. For example, the surprising result of the Michelson-Morley experiment, that there is no difference in the speed of electromagnetic waves in any direction, is borne out by the special theory of relativity, specifically the rejection of the hypothesis of the aether and of absolute motion.[3] Rather than being undermined by presupposed concepts, the experiment and its theoretical explanation serve to undermine inadequate scientific concepts such as those of the aether and of absolute motion. Yet, these concepts, especially that of the aether (αἰθήρ), are not without philosophical connections; thus, their undermining has consequences also for philosophy. This connection is indicative of the complex intertwining of scientific advances and philosophical conceptuality. Scientific advances may recoil on philosophical concepts and thereby pose the requirement that these concepts be put in question. Philosophy, in turn, can legitimately require that certain scientific concepts be interrogated as regards their ground and their precise determination.

* * *

It is self-evident: there could be no filled space if there were no space as such to be filled. That space as such has no separate existence means, not that space has no existence whatsoever, but that space is always filled, that it never occurs in the form of empty space. It is not that there is no such thing as empty space but that space, while indeed existing, is always filled.

The differentiation between space as such and filled space corresponds to that between luminous space and the space of self-showing. Yet, this correspondence is limited; it is not a matter of identity. For, in the first place, that which fills space is not necessarily a thing: it may be something that shows itself indirectly or by means of a technical receptor; it may even be something that does not show itself at all, as in the case of a black hole. Furthermore, the differentiation between luminous space and the space of self-showing is not a matter of filling at all. Rather, it is the conclusion of a series of determinations that constitute a genesis involving also the natural elementals and the constitution of place. The space of self-showing is the final determination of luminous space, the final term of the genesis, whereas in the differentiation between space as such and filled space there is no course of determinations.

It is because there is always something that fills space that space, though itself invisible, can display a kind of visibility. Such a display is most manifest

---

3. "But all experiments have shown that electro-magnetic and optical phenomena, relatively to the earth as the body of reference, are not influenced by the translational velocity of the earth. The most important of these experiments are those of Michelson and Morley, which I shall assume are known. The validity of the principle of special relativity can therefore hardly be doubted" (ibid., 26–27).

when that which is in space is a surrogate that in its movement traces the space in question and thereby offers an intimation of the space itself.

In the cosmos there are things that, while they occupy space, are no less invisible than space itself. Yet, they occupy space in a manner quite different from that of ordinary matter or even that of cosmic microwave background radiation. They represent a thorough alteration of the normal filling of space, and thereby they are constituted as invisible in a previously inconceivable sense. They are withdrawn from visibility; they have always already retreated from visibility.

Such a retreat from visibility in the cosmic abode is exemplified by what is termed *dark matter*. That dark matter actually exists is a supposition based on the analysis of the dynamics of galaxies. Observation-based research shows that in the rotation of the Milky Way the orbital velocities of bodies at various distances from the center of the galaxy are approximately the same. It can be shown that this invariance would not be possible if the rotation were determined solely by the gravitational attraction of the stars in the galaxy along with other visible material such as gas and dust. In more specific terms, if the hydrogen clouds beyond the edge of the galaxy were subject only to the gravitational pull of the visible stars in the galaxy, their velocity should fall off roughly according to the square root of their distance outside the visible limits of the galaxy. Yet, the fact that the velocity remains almost constant implies that the outer gas is subject to the gravitational pull of a larger mass than that exerted by the stars within the galaxy.[4] The only solution seems to be that there is a huge spherical halo of dark—that is, invisible—matter that surrounds the entire galaxy and contributes massively to the determination of the rotation. While this matter thus exerts gravity, it must be such that it does not interact with light or any other form of radiation; hence, dark matter can consist neither of ordinary stars nor of the interstellar gas that emits X-rays. Calculation shows that this dark matter is as much as seven times the mass of the visible bodies in the Milky Way. And yet, it is widely agreed that the nature of dark matter is unknown, though some recent research provides evidence—though still quite hypothetical—that strange particles such as neutrinos may constitute a few percent of the mass of dark matter. Yet, neutrinos are hardly more accessible to research than dark matter itself. They rarely interact with matter, and thus it is extremely difficult to detect them, since even the most sensitive instruments are based on such interaction.[5] Only in 2015 was it demonstrated that neutrinos actually have mass; the demonstration was based on the discovery that neutrinos oscillate between different types, and the knowledge

---

4. See Mitchell Begelman and Martin Rees, *Gravity's Fatal Attraction* (Cambridge: Cambridge University Press, 2010), 79.
5. See ibid., 90–91.

that such oscillation is possible only if they have mass. Because they have mass, they can account for some of the dark matter in the universe, though only for a small percentage.

In the case of black holes the retreat of visibility becomes absolute. It is as though black holes were an inversion, negation, or withdrawal of space as determined most rigorously by Kant and by Hegel. For Kant, space is exteriority: in order to be able to represent something outside us, "the representation of space must be presupposed. . . . Outer experience is itself possible at all only through that representation." Or again: "Space is a necessary *a priori* representation that underlies all outer intuitions [*äusseren Anschauungen*]."[6] In other words, space is the condition for externality as such. Space must already be there, must indeed constitute the *there*, in order for something to appear there as outside, as external. Space is nothing but the representation of exteriority, the condition under which outer things can be experienced, can be intuited as exterior.

For Hegel, too, space is the form of exteriority. He describes it in terms of the *here*: each *here* constitutes a point in space, which is entirely absolved from all relation to any other *here*[7]—that is, it is wholly exterior to every other *here*. On the other hand, all *heres* are, as Hegel says, "completely the same."[8] Hence, there is no mediation whatsoever, no connection between the *heres*; each is simply exterior to all others. In Hegel's idiom, it can be said that space is merely "abstract plurality," a plurality in which there is no connection, no mediation, no structure, that would bring the *heres* into relation. Space is pure exteriority.

Inversely, a black hole is pure interiority. It has no outside except that which serves to cancel all exteriority.

A star is normally sustained in an equilibrium by a balance between the inward attraction of the star's gravity and the outward force produced by the pressure in the star's hot interior resulting from the nuclear fusion primarily of hydrogen into helium. Once the nuclear fuel (hydrogen and the successively heavier elements up to iron) is exhausted, the gravitational force brings about the collapse of the star. Because of the enormous density developed in the core, the protons and electrons are fused to form neutrons, and if its mass does not exceed three solar masses, the result is a neutron star; otherwise it is a black hole. One distinctive difference between a neutron star and a black hole is that a neutron star has real surfaces, whereas a black hole has only a horizon and no physical surface at all.

In the formation of a black hole, the outer layer of the star is blown off as a supernova, while the core contracts until its density—hence, its gravitational

---

6. Kant, *Kritik der reinen Vernunft*, A23/B38.
7. Hegel, *Enzyklopädie der philosophischen Wissenschaften*, §254; 260 *Zusatz*.
8. Hegel, §254 *Zusatz*.

force—is so enormous that nothing can escape from it, not even light. The black hole that is thus formed is centered in—draws itself toward—a point termed a singularity, which defines the most interior of the interior. The region around the black hole, from which nothing can escape, is termed the event-horizon. Since light cannot escape beyond the event-horizon, the black hole is invisible, absolutely, irresolvably invisible.[9] Its invisibility is of a kind unmatched by those forms belonging to ordinary things (their profile-structure, for instance) and even by that of dark matter, which could, in principle, be made visible. With black holes the retreat of visibility reaches its absolute limit. The identity that, with only rare exceptions, philosophical discourse has posited between being and presence, between that which *is* and that which can be brought to presence, that which can be rendered perceptually present—or specifically, visible—before the perceiver, is completely cancelled by the occurrence of black holes. The concept of being must now be expanded to take account of the nonpresence and nonvisibility of black holes. This is perhaps the most decisive reorientation that philosophical discourse must undergo as a result of an astronomical discovery.

As the monstrously dense, absolutely invisible core of a star, a black hole is neither a hole nor is it black.

Many black holes spin (they are termed Kerr black holes). As a black hole spins, it swirls extremely hot gas around it, especially at its equator. This vortex of hot gas is termed the accretion disk. As the gas is swirled around, some will escape and then is ejected in twin jets of particles, which can extend for enormous distances. Observation of the accretion disk and of these jets provides one of the ways in which the existence of a black hole can be detected. Another principal way is by observing its gravitational effect on neighboring bodies.

Yet, black holes can be most effectively detected and measured in binary systems where the black hole captures and draws into its accretion disk matter from its companion star. As the accretion disk swirls around the event-horizon, it can be determined how the inner edge of the disk has changed in size and shape as the black hole has consumed material from it. As the gas belonging to the material consumed from the companion star reaches the innermost region of the accretion disk just outside the event-horizon, it pulses; by timing the pulsations the mass of the black hole can be determined.

Set within its event-horizon and its accretion disk and drawing itself toward its singularity, a black hole is pure interiority. Its would-be visibility has always retreated into this interior.

---

9. It has been noted that the general theory of relativity allows that there could be white holes, that is, regions of space that cannot be entered from the outside and yet allow light and matter to escape. Such holes have not been observed. For the context of such a supposition, see Chris Impey, *Einstein's Monsters* (New York: W. W. Norton, 2019), 22–23.

As pure interiority, a black hole is, as such, absolute in a sense akin to that expressed in philosophical discourse; both black holes and the philosophical absolute are absolved from all dependence, all essential relations, to anything outside themselves. A black hole is structurally analogous to the self-relation by which the absolute of philosophical discourse is determined: for a black hole draws itself to itself, toward a point that would be the most interior of the interior.

The evidence is that there are millions of black holes in the Milky Way, many with a mass many times that of the sun, and that there are supermassive black holes in the center of most galaxies.

As such, they install within the cosmic abode negativities of a unique kind. They are not resolvable in the sense conveyed by the expression "Turning nothing into being"; that is, they do not submit to dialectic. The negativity is rather one of retreat and, in the case of black holes, a retreat into absolute, irrevocable invisibility.

* * *

As the broadest, indeed ultimate abode, the cosmos and the self-understanding it offers have a distinctive significance. If one listens carefully to Hegel's observation that "No matter how remotely I place a star, I can go beyond it, for the world is nowhere nailed up with boards,"[10] one can hear in this observation an understanding that the cosmos offers humans no stabilizing *terminus*, that there is also no center, no pervasive structure gathering up all things into at least the semblance of a whole, as one in fact finds in the other abodes. To be sure, there are structures, mammoth structures, in space: clusters of galaxies, for example, and supervoids. Yet, these are structures that offer little, if any, orientation to humans—for instance, in the way that the institutions in a city serve as orienting structures for the citizens.

As one looks out into the cosmos, perhaps using the latest technical resources, in full awareness of present-day knowledge of the cosmos, one may articulate one's self-understanding in various ways. Lacking structures and a center that might provide humans with a modicum of orientation, the cosmos can appear as like a boundless ocean on which one is—for better or for worse—set adrift. Or it may appear as the site of gigantic forms that so exceed the human that almost no measure of this excess is in human terms possible: a star in the constellation Scutum that is seventeen hundred times the diameter of our sun; a star in a companion galaxy to the Milky Way that is 8.7 million times brighter than our sun, emitting as much energy in four seconds as the sun does in a year; and jets of gas that are expelled by spinning black holes and travel at speeds very close to

---

10. Hegel, *Enzyklopädie der philosophischen Wissenschaften*, §254 Zusatz.

the speed of light. And if these appearances seem to render humankind ever less significant, there is also reason to celebrate the wonder and the vision by which humans are able to bring all this to appear, each in the way appropriate to it.

Humans can bring to appear all that belongs to ethicality, that is, the configuration of the nest of abodes and the proper elements in their bond to the proper self. These moments of ethicality are brought to appear by force of imagination, which opens a space within which these moments are luminously presented. Not only art but also other engagements—cosmology's unlimitable mapping of the vast expanse of the cosmos and, at the other extreme, its discovery of black holes as withdrawing into the utmost intimacy—possess the dynamism by which mortality, natality, seclusion, as well as the projection of polities and of being with others and with nature are enticed into surrendering their truth. It is by way of such disclosures that ethical self-understanding can be achieved.

The cosmos can also speak into one's solitude, sounding—if silently—across the great expanse between it and the proximal abode of the self. Once again recall what Emerson writes of solitude and of the heavens: "To go into solitude, a man needs to retire as much from his chamber as from society. I am not solitary whilst I read and write, though nobody is with me. But if a man would be alone, let him look at the stars."

Index

JOHN SALLIS is Frederick J. Adelmann Professor of Philosophy at Boston College. He is author of more than twenty-five books, including *Force of Imagination*, *Logic of Imagination*, *Chorology*, *Songs of Nature*, and *On Beauty and Measure*. He is a Senior Fellow at the Freiburg Institute for Advanced Studies and has held positions as Visiting Professor at numerous universities. In addition, he is the recipient of the Alexander von Humboldt Research Prize and holds an honorary doctorate from the University of Freiburg. His writings have been translated into more than a dozen languages. He is the founding editor of the journal *Research in Phenomenology*. Moreover, he has actively contributed to various studies and events pertaining to modern art and, in particular, has curated two major exhibitions at the McMullen Museum of Art in Boston, one devoted to the paintings and drawings of Paul Klee and the other focusing on the landscapes of Cao Jun.

CPSIA information can be obtained
at www.ICGtesting.com
Printed in the USA
LVHW111734190922
728750LV00004B/424